Raspberry Pi 3

A Practical Beginner's Guide To Understanding The Full Potential Of Raspberry Pi 3 By Starting Your Own Projects Using Python Programming

Finn Sanders

Table of Contents

Introduction 6

Chapter 1: The Basics of Raspberry Pi 3 10

The Specifications 13

The Different Versions of Raspberry Pi 14

The Operating System 19

Raspbian 21

The Benefits of Working with Raspberry Pi 24

Chapter 2: How to Set Up Your Raspberry Pi 3........ 33

What Do I Need to Know to Get Started? 34

The First Step: Installing Your Operating System 36

Hooking Up the Raspberry Pi Device 39

Getting the Raspbian Operating System Set Up...40

Configuring Your Raspberry Pi............................ 43

Connecting to the Wi-Fi in Your Home 44

Connecting to the Bluetooth devices 45

Can I Connect with the Raspberry Pi 3 Device in a Remote Manner? 47

Chapter 3: A Look at How to Navigate Through the Menus, Folders, and Files of

Raspberry Pi 3 50
Important Files 51
Navigating the Menus in a Desktop Environment 54
Chapter 4: Using the IDLE Editor to Write Your Own Python Programs 58
The Process of Writing the Code Directly into the Console 64
The Process of Writing the Code to a Document 66
Writing Comments in Python 67
Chapter 5: Some Basics of Writing the Python Code 70
Regular Expressions 71
Doing the Queries in Python 76
Loops 80
Working with Inheritances 91
Chapter 6: Using the Raspberry Pi 97
Ways to Interface the Electronics 97
The Communication Protocols 101
Real-Time Interfacing Using Arduino 104
Input and Output 106
Capturing Images, Audio, and Videos 106

Chapter 7: How to Use GPIO Pins for Your Device.......... 115
An Example of How This Works.......... 118
Chapter 8: Tips and Tricks to Get the Most Out of Your Raspberry Pi.......... 120
Download Chromium.......... 121
Work with a Script Blocker.......... 121
Try to Limit How Many Things Are Running at a Time.......... 123
Don't Worry About a Big Keyboard or Monitor.......... 124
Use the Raspberry Pi as a Virtual Assistant.......... 126
Flash Photography Could Reset the Pi.......... 127
Try Out Some of the Projects.......... 128
Learn a Coding Language.......... 129
Chapter 9: How to Install a Heat Sink.......... 131
The Process of Installing the Heat Sink.......... 134
Chapter 10: How to Create Your Own Arcade Box.......... 142
Chapter 11: Can I Turn My Raspberry Pi 3 into a Phone?.......... 151
Chapter 12: Turning the Raspberry Pi into a Media Server.......... 158

Ways to Store the Media 164
Chapter 13: The Best Accessories for Raspberry Pi 3 to Make It Work Better 168
Breadboard 169
The Raspberry Pi Heat Sink 171
The Raspberry Pi Camera Module 172
The Raspberry Pi Case 174
Raspberry Pi Displays 176
The Raspberry Pi CanaKit 177
Chapter 14: The LED Project 181
Building the Circuit 185
Writing the Program 187
Chapter 15: Creating a Photo Frame 192
Chapter 16: Installing a Magic Mirror on the Raspberry Pi 3 199
Chapter 17: Troubleshooting Your Raspberry Pi Device 206
Ways to Avoid an SD Card That Is Corrupted 208
How to Avoid Relying on Only the Main Power 210
Checking out the Cables That You Are Using 212
Conclusion 216

Introduction

The following chapters will discuss everything that you need to know to get started with the Raspberry Pi 3 device. There are a lot of changes that are always coming up in the world of technology. Many people want to join in and learn more about this technology and about programming, but they feel that it is just too complicated for them to understand. The Raspberry Pi 3 helps anyone to learn how to code and program and will ensure that you are going to be able to do some neat things with technology all on your own.

If you have ever wanted to learn how to work with technology, and even how to get started with programming, but felt a little worried that it was going to be too difficult for you to learn, then this guidebook is the tool for you. Raspberry Pi makes it easy for anyone to learn how to program, and this guidebook will show you the step by step process that you need to follow to start your own adventure into the world of technology.

This guidebook is going to take some time to discuss the Raspberry Pi 3 and some of the neat things that you can do with it. We will first discuss what the Raspberry Pi 3 is all about and how it is different compared to some of the earlier versions of Raspberry Pi. We will look at some of the operating systems and some of the coding languages that will work the best with this code. We can then explore how to work with the Python language to program this device, how to get into your files and get them set up, and some tips to ensure that you can really get the most out of this device.

We will also spend some time in this guidebook looking at some of the different projects that you can create when you are working on your Raspberry Pi device. We will look at how to turn this device into an arcade, how to turn it into a phone, and even how to make the Raspberry Pi into your own media device for the whole family to use. The possibilities of what you can do using this device are endless, and we only had time for a few of them inside. But anything that you can imagine, or would like to create, is possible if you have the Raspberry Pi, some coding language, and the right accessories to help you get started.

There are so many things that you are able to do and enjoy about this Raspberry Pi 3 device. It is the perfect way for a beginner to learn a bit more about programming and to ensure that you are going to be able to get some of the basics down before you move on to some more complex programming and coding projects. When you are ready to get started with Raspberry Pi and want to be able to use it like a pro, make sure to check out this guidebook to help you get started!

Chapter 1: The Basics of Raspberry Pi 3

There are a lot of neat things available in technology today—from many programming languages to choose from to all the different items that you can go with as well. With all of the changes, though, many of those who are beginners or who have no experience working with any of the coding or programming may feel like they are getting left behind in the process, or they may worry that the work is just too much for them to learn.

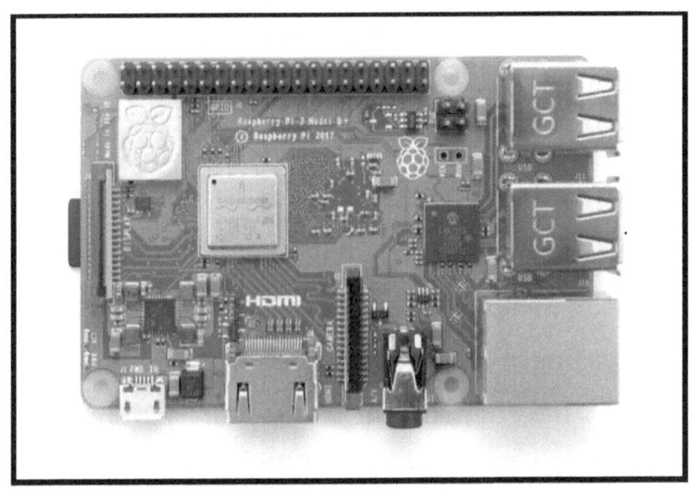

Source: Raspberry Pi [ONLINE]. Available at: https://en.wikipedia.org/wiki/Raspberry_Pi [Accessed 28 March 2019]

Raspberry Pi 3 is a way to help solve this problem. This is a little credit card-sized computer that is able to connect to your TV or to your computer monitor. It is a smaller device, but very powerful, and provides people of all ages a way to explore how the world of computers work and can help them learn how to program in many different languages such as Scratch and Python. It is much easier to use than a lot of the other programming tools out there and provides a safe way for these new programmers to work on their own skills.

The Raspberry Pi 3 device is capable of doing anything that you would expect your regular desktop computer to do, such as gaming, processing voices, creating tables, playing videos in HD, internet searches, and more. Even more, this device also has the ability to interact with the outside world. There have been a lot of digital projects made with this device—from detectors for parents, musical instruments, homes for birds with infra-red cameras, and even meteorological stations.

As you can see, there are a lot of parts that come with the Raspberry Pi 3, and there are many different projects that you can choose to work on. We will take a look at some of the different options that you can create later in this guidebook. It is amazing how such a little device, one that looks so simple, can make a big difference in how well you can learn about computers and how easy programming and coding languages can be.

The Specifications

Even though the Raspberry Pi 3 is a smaller device, there are a lot of components present that you will enjoy this small computer. The Raspberry Pi 3 is the third generation of Raspberry Pi, and the main differences that you are going to see with this version compared to the older versions include:

1.2 GHz 64-bit quad-core ARMv8 CPU
802.11n Wireless LAN
Bluetooth 4.1
Bluetooth Low Energy

In addition to some of the changes between

Raspberry Pi 3 and the earlier versions, there are a few other components that you are going to enjoy when you use this product. These include:

VideoCore IV 3D graphics core
Micro SD card slot
Display interface
Camera interface
Combined 3.5-mm audio jack with composite video
Ethernet port
Full HDMI port
40 GPIO pins
4 USB ports
1 GB RAM

The Different Versions of Raspberry Pi

There are actually a few different versions of Raspberry Pi out there. While Raspberry Pi 3 is one of the newest versions of this program, and it can often do some of the more advanced things that you are looking at, there are other models that come in with different features and different price points depending on what you want to get out of the system. Some of the different models that you are able to choose from with Raspberry Pi include:

Raspberry PI 1 Model A: This Model A version is the original that came out in 2012. The Plus version of this came out a few years later and was an improvement because it had a larger hard drive and the price point came in lower than the previous version.

Raspberry Pi 2 Model B: The first generation of this came out in 2012, and then the Plus model came out in 2014. The Plus version of the Model B came in with a lower price, and it allowed the user to work with a microSD slot rather than relying on the standard SD slot that was in previous versions.

Raspberry Pi Zero: This model of the Raspberry Pi family came out in 2015. The Zero was designed to be smaller than some of the other versions, and this resulted in reduced output and input for the user. However, it is the least expensive of the Raspberry Pi's, which made it more affordable than ever. When the Zero originally came out, it didn't have any video input options. But in 2016, there was a second version of this released that had this feature.

Raspberry Pi 2: This is the model that have a lot more features compared to any of the models that came out before. It was released in early 2015, and the model is considered one of the higher end versions from this family. Even though it is higher-end, it is still very affordable, coming in at just $35.

Raspberry Pi 3: This is the newest model of this computer family. It was released in early 2016, and it comes bundled with all the additions that you need in order to really get things going with this computer. Some of the accessories that are often sold with this model include USB boot capabilities, Bluetooth, and Wi-Fi.

These are just a few of the options when it comes to working with Raspberry Pi. Even though you can choose from a few different option, you will find that some of the features are going to be considered pretty standard between them all. For example, you will find that all of them are going to have a Broadcom on a chip, and their central processing system is compatible with the ARM protocol. There is going to be a GPU on these systems as well.

Every board is going to come with a slot for at least one USB, though some of them will come with two, three, and even four of these slots for you to use. You should also be able to find slots on this for phone jacks, HDMI, and composite video output to help with any of the audio work that you wish to complete.

The good news is that the team who has worked to create and develop many of the Raspberry Pi models that you have come to know and love are also the ones that have created the Raspbian operating system to help users work with the system. The Raspbian operating system is similar to what you can find with Linux, so if you have used that operating system in the past, you are going to catch on to Raspbian really quickly.

You will also find that you can work with other operating systems on this computer if you wish. You can work with Ubuntu, Windows 10, RISC OS and more depending on what you are the most comfortable with, and what works the best for your project.

The Operating System

To get the device up and running in the proper manner so that you can use it, there needs to be some kind of operating system in place. While this may seem like a lot of work and a challenge, the best approach to use is to pick out some kind of operating system that is going to suit the tasks that you plan to use with the Raspberry Pi 3.

There are actually quite a few operating systems that will work on this device, which means that you can get a lot of freedom in the choice that you make. If you are a beginner, you may find that the best operating system to work with is either Python or Raspbian. Some of the other operating systems that are popular and can be customized to work well with the Raspberry Pi 3 device includes:

- **Raspbian**: This is the official operating system that is supported by this device.

- **Pidora**: This is a Fedora Remix operating system that has been changed a bit, so it works well with Raspberry Pi.

- **RaspBMC**: This is a free and open sourced media center. If you plan to use the device just for that, then this is a good operating system to choose.

- **OpenELEC**: This is a Linux based operating system that is a bit smaller, so it works better on the device. It is able to turn your Raspberry Pi into a Kodi media center.

- **RISC OS**: This is an operating system that is very compact, which makes it fast. This one has been designed in a way that works the best on devices with ARM architecture.

- **Arch**: This is going to be a flexible and a lightweight Linux distribution that you can work with.

- **Python**: Python is one of the best programming languages that you can work with as a beginner. We will take a look at some of the coding that you should know to about when it comes to using Python so you can write your own codes on this device.

Raspbian

Along with Python, Raspbian is the most popular of the operating systems to use on these Raspberry Pi devices. This operating system is going to be completely free to use so you won't have to worry about any added costs, and it is going to be based on Debian. It is going to represent a set of programs and utilities that will help you ensure that your devices are going to run properly.

You will find that Raspbian isn't just going to work for you as an operating system. It is also going to come with more than 35,000 packages in a format that makes them easier to install. The Raspbian operating system is always going through improvements each day, and there is still a lot of activity in terms of development, which means that it is just going to get better and better.

This operating system is going to come with an environment that works on a desktop, so it looks very similar to some of the operating systems that you are used to working with already. In addition, you will be able to work with the menus that are present in order to get all of the active programs to do the work. Using this desktop environment can be nice for those who aren't used to working with the Linux console so far.

Keep in mind that this device is not going to have enough power, and it is not going to be strong enough, to do some of the bigger processes that we are used to finishing with desktop computers. This means that doing photography, video editing, and watching some 4K movies. But there are still a lot of things that you will be able to do with this little computer, and you will be amazed at what the Raspbian operating system is able to do.

Since Raspbian is a distribution of Linux, you can feel better knowing that your programs are going to have some good security features, and the network capabilities are going to be high. Linux is a great option for an operating system, and you will be able to get a lot of the different projects done with this little computer. You can also work with the other operating systems if you want, depending on the needs of your projects.

There are so many different things that you can do with the Raspberry Pi computer. Even though it is a small little computer, you will be amazed at all of the things that you are able to get done with this, and all of the cool things that come with this. It is the perfect addition to helping anyone learn more about technology and how to get some of the big projects done for their own needs in no time.

The Benefits of Working with Raspberry Pi

There are a lot of different options that you are able to choose to use when you are trying to learn how programming works. And many of these are going to be great at getting the work done. But sometimes, the other options are going to seem a little bit intimidating to someone who is a beginner with the whole process.

This is where the Raspberry Pi family comes in. It is a small computer that allows you to do a lot of different programming and coding tasks, in a way that is more user-friendly and easier to work with. There are a lot of benefits that come to using this Raspberry Pi device, and those include:

1) Power consumption: The Raspberry Pi family of products isn't going to take up a lot of electricity to get things done. In fact, Pi is only going to draw in somewhere between five and seven watts of electricity. This is actually about a tenth of what a comparable full-size box can use. Since the servers are running all the time, this savings is going to add up really quickly. This saves you a lot of energy, and a lot of money, while still being able to do a lot of

the same tasks in the process.

2) The parts don't move. The nice thing here is that the Pi device is going to rely on an SD card for storage. This is a fast method of storage, and it isn't going to have any moving parts. There are also no fans or other similar parts that you have to worry about. In many cases, you will find that working with an SD card that is Class 10 is going to be the best performance for you compared to some of the lower class cards.

3) Small form factor. The Pi, along with the case, is easily held in your hand. Think about that! You can fit a whole computer in your hand, and it still allows you to play games, turn it in different devices, and do all of the programming and more that you want to do. A comparable full-size box, which does a lot of the same things, can't fit

into your hand. What this means, outside of just being convenient, is that you can take the Pi device and integrate it inside of other devices as well.

4) No noise: When you think about one of your traditional computers, you may notice that there is a lot of noise that comes with it. For some big box computers, this noise is going to be insanely loud. But when you are working with one of the Pi devices, you will quickly notice that despite all of the power behind it, there isn't any noise to worry about.

5) Status lights. When you are working with the motherboard of the device, you will notice that there are several status lights there. And when you choose to work with a clear case, you will be able to see these status lights to check on the power status,

the disk I/O, and the NIC activity.

6) The ability to expand out: There are a lot of devices that are available for you to use with Pi, and many of them are going to be affordable enough that you can try a few of them out. You can find ways to expand this product including the camera, the I/O board and more. And the Pi is going to come with two USB ports to help with expansion. But there is also the option to hook up a powered USB hub so that you can add on as many devices as you want.

7) Built-in HDMI capable graphics: The display port that comes on these devices is going to be HDMI, which means that it is going to be able to handle resolutions up to 1920 by 1200. This is a great thing because it ensures that you are able to do a lot of things with the device, including turning it

into a video player box. There are also a few converters that you can work with that will help you to use VGA with backward compatibility.

8) Affordable: When you look at a lot of the different options for technology that are out there right now, you will find that they are very expensive. But when you compare the Pi device with some of the others, you will find that it comes with the best specs for the price. It is one of the few devices in its class that is able to offer you with 512 MB of RAM. The Pi has even gone down in price since it first arrived, and it is something that is really affordable as business use, hobby, or whatever need there is.

9) A lot of support in the community: The Pi has phenomenal community support. This support can be obtained quite easily for the

hardware and the Linux software that runs on the Pi mainly in user forums, depending on the GNU/Linux distribution used.

10) Overclocking capability: The Pi device can be overclocked if there are some problems with the performance with the application used, but it is at the risk of the user to try and do this.

11) Lots of different uses. You will find that since you are able to keep the storage that you need on the SD card makes it easy to swap with other SD cards. This makes it easier for you to quickly and easily change the functionality of the device—if you want to set up the Pi to run as a server to test it out—and then you can just swap out the SD card and try out something different. And when you are done, you are able to use the "*dd*" command on your computer—you can

do a backup of the SD card and keep it for restoration later if you would like.

With all of the positives that come with the Raspberry Pi, it may seem like there are no negatives and that you should jump right in. However, there are a few things that may be considered drawbacks when it comes to using this device.

1) The first drawback is that it relies on ARM architectures. While ARM can be considered a low powered and highly efficient architecture, it is not going to be x86, and this means that any of the binaries that are compiled and ready to run on the x86 are not going to run with Pi. The good news here is that the GNU and Linux distributions are compiled to work with the ARM architecture, and there are always big changes coming up to help as well. And

there aren't that many projects and applications that only work with x86 so you should be fine.

2) Another issue is that the RAM on this device is not going to be upgradable. The main components of the Pi device are going to be soldered together in the motherboard, which includes the RAM at 512 MB. This is not a big problem because you can easily run the GNU and Linux on them. If you aren't running the X11, you will see that the Pi device is going to rely on 100 MB of RAM, which still leaves you plenty of room for other things.

Chapter 2: How to Set Up Your Raspberry Pi 3

Now that we know a little bit more about Raspberry Pi 3, it is time to learn how to get this device hooked up and ready-to-go. There are a few steps that you will need to take in order to ensure that this device is going to work the way that you want and that you can see some great results. We are going to take a look at how you can set up the operating system properly, how to get it all set up, and even how to test out the program to make sure that it works and is ready to do the projects and other work that you would like it to.

What Do I Need to Know to Get Started?

Before we start on this process, there are going to be certain supplies that you need to purchase—or make sure that you have on hand—before you see success. To start, you need to have your Raspberry Pi 3 device ready-to-use. The other supplies that you may find helpful when you are setting up this device include:

A monitor or television that can take HDMI: You will need to be able to connect the device to some sort of display. A television or your computer monitor is fine as long as they can handle HDMI. There are also some compact options that you can choose to work with if you wish.

A mouse and a keyboard: These need to be connected to a USB so that they can hook into the Raspberry Pi. Any type will work to get this done, but they need to hook in so that you can give the device some instructions.

MicroSD card and its card reader: The operating system that comes with the Raspberry Pi does not use a hard drive. Instead, it comes with a MicroSD card already installed. Make sure that you get one that has at least 8GB, or you won't be able to do much with the device. If your personal computer might have a card reader so if you are using that, you are probably set. However, if the screen you are using doesn't have this, you can find a card reader online for about $10.

Power supply: The Raspberry device is going to be powered through a micro USB. This is similar to what your phone runs on. There are four USB ports to supply power to. Just make sure that the power supply that you choose is able to give a minimum of 2.5A of power to the device.

Once you have all of these parts in place and

ready to use, it is time to get started with setting up your Raspberry Pi 3 devices.

The First Step: Installing Your Operating System

After all of the supplies are ready for you to use them, the first part of the process of setting up your Raspberry Pi 3 is to make sure that the operating system is put on. We are going to focus on getting the Raspbian operating system loaded up and making sure that it works well on the memory card so that you can use the device.

To work on this, you will need to make sure that you have a laptop or desktop computer to work with. The Raspbian operating system will need to have you load it on a regular computer of some kind. You can then put it on your SD card and transfer it over to the Raspberry Pi 3 device when you are ready.

Now, there are some choices here, and you can pick from two. First, it is possible to go through and make sure that the Raspbian operating system is manually installed on your system. This means that you will need to work with either some external software to do it—or you have to have enough experience in coding to get the work done by typing it into the command line.

The second option that you can work with, and the one that a lot of people like to go with because it's seen as easier, is to download and install NOOBs. Since this is the option that a lot of people favor because they find it easier to do, some of the steps that you need to do in order to download and then install the NOOBs includes:

Take the SD card that you plan to use inside a card reader or your computer.

On that same computer, take the time to download NOOBs. There should be several options for you to choose from here. Go with "*offline and network install*". This is the option that includes Raspbian right in the download.

In some cases, the SD card needs to be formatted as FAT. If this ends up being the case with your card, then you can download the formatting tool from the SD Association, which you should find at sdcard.org. From here, you can look for the part "Format Size Adjustment". Make sure that part is on in your options menu and then the card is ready.

You should end up with a Zip file. You can extract it here. Once this is done, make sure to copy all the contents of the folder over to the SD card. When you are done copying, take the SD card out of the card reader or the computer and insert it back into the Raspberry device.

Hooking Up the Raspberry Pi Device

Now that we have gotten some of the work with the operating system all done, it is time to make sure that all of the devices that you will use with the Raspberry Pi device are hooked and connected to it. This is a simple step because you will just take all of the parts and plug them into the USB ports that are on the Raspberry Pi.

However, you will find that following a particular order is going to be a better option when you are doing it. This method is the best because it will ensure that each of the devices that you connect to the Raspberry Pi will be recognized when you boot up. The order that you will want to use to ensure that this all works in your favor includes:

- Start by connecting the monitor to the device.

- When the monitor is recognized, you can connect the keyboard and the mouse as well.

- If you want to work with an Ethernet cable in order to get your internet, then this is the time to connect it.

- And finally, connect the power that you are using. Since this device doesn't come with a power switch, as soon as that power source gets plugged into the device, then the device will turn on.

Getting the Raspbian Operating System Set Up

When you are ready, it is time to boot up the NOOBs that we were talking about earlier. This can take a few minutes to load up, so you may not see anything happen right away. This is because the NOOBs program is taking its time working on formatting the SD card that you choose, and checking that all of the other parts are set up in the proper manner.

Don't get impatient here. Even though you are excited to get the device to work well and you want it up and running right now to use, take your time and let the NOOBs do the tasks that it needs. If you rush through this or try to skip ahead, it is going to cause a lot of bigger problems to the system later on.

After the few minutes have passed, you will notice that there is a screen that shows up. This screen should ask you to install the operating system that you are looking to use on the device. You can pick from any operating system that you want. But we are going to take a look at the steps that you need to download and use Raspbian. Some of the steps you need to do this will include:

- Look towards the bottom of your console screen. There should be a place there where you are able to select the keyboard layout, as well as the language, based on your region.

- Look for the Raspbian operating system and then check that box. This tells the system to install the operating system.

- NOOBs will take on the work to install this operating system. This does take a little bit to complete, up to 20 minutes, so be patient. When the Raspbian operating system is uploaded, you will be taken to the desktop for Raspbian, and you can configure everything else that you need.

Configuring Your Raspberry Pi

At this point, your Raspberry Pi device is pretty much ready-to-go. You are able to take a look at the operating system and see that the start menu is in place. There are a few more steps that we need to take a look at to see the best results with this device, and you will need to go over to the start menu in order to get the setup finished.

From your start menu, you need to select the application, and then click on open a file browser. From here, you will be able to enter any of the commands that you want and tell the system what you would like to do. This is similar to what we see with other operating systems. We will take a look at some of the commands that you can use with this in a bit.

There are a few other options that you need to work on when you want to get the Raspberry Pi device up and running. We are going to take some time to look at how to install and set up the Wi-Fi, the Bluetooth, and more so that you can get the most out of this device.

Connecting to the Wi-Fi in Your Home

The good news is that it is pretty easy to use Raspbian in order to get the Raspberry Pi device hooked up to the Wi-Fi in your home. In fact, you are going to follow pretty much the same steps as you would when you are hooking your regular computer up to the Wi-Fi.

The first thing that you will do is look for the network icon on your main menu and click on it. This is going to be the icon that looks like there are two computers next to each other. You should be able to find it on the top right-hand side of your screen. Once you find that icon, you can click on it and search or the Wi-Fi that you use at home. Click on that and enter the password that comes with it.

And that is all that you will need to do. If you have the right Wi-Fi network and the right password in place, you will find that the Raspbian operating system will be able to go through and hook the Raspberry Pi device up with your Wi-Fi, allowing you to do some of the other things that you need with the system. Once you make the connection with the network, the device is going to automatically hook back up with the Wi-Fi each time that you need it.

Connecting to the Bluetooth devices

There may be some times when you decide that you want to allow the Raspberry Pi 3 device to hook up with a mouse or a keyboard that is enabled through Bluetooth. If this is something that you are interested in doing, then you will need to spend a bit of time now, or at a later time, pairing them together. Depending on the device that you are looking to pair, the process is going to have variations to it. Some of the simple steps that you can use to make this work for your needs include.

First, go onto the screen and check where the icon for Bluetooth is. Click on the icon that is near the top of your screen. Once you have clicked on the icon, you can look for the option to Add Device. Click there, and then search through the different options that are available there. Find the one that you wish to pair with the device and then follow the directions that show up on the screen to help you finish up the process.

And that is all there is to it. Just by doing a simple search and clicking on the right things, you will be able to get any Bluetooth enabled device hooked up to your Pi device. Once they are synced up, you can start to get it to work just like you would on a regular computer.

Can I Connect with the Raspberry Pi 3 Device in a Remote Manner?

Now, there are going to be some instances when you are working with your Raspberry Pi 3, and you find that you need to be able to get onto this device remotely. Perhaps, at the time, you aren't able to get ahold of a monitor near you, or you just want to be able to get to the Pi device even if it isn't right next to you. The good news is that just like with a regular computer—you are able to do this with a few different options including:

Use the command line to connect: You are able to use SSH from any computer in your home. This allows you to get ahold of the interface for command lines on the Raspberry Pi. While this option means that you can't access a graphic interface, you would instead be able to run any command that you want through the Terminal. When the command is sent through the Terminal, it is going to execute on the Raspberry Pi 3. This is a useful thing to try out any time that you have a project that doesn't really need a screen to get the work done.

Work with VNC to make another computer the remote screen: If you need to access the Raspberry Pi remotely and you need to work with the graphical interface, then the virtual network computing, or the VNC, is the best bet. You will then be able to see the desktop from the Raspberry device on your computer desktop and then control it as needed. This option is kind of slow so you shouldn't use it all the time. But for occasional use to make things easier, it can be a great option.

When you end up at this point, you should have the Raspberry Pi device all set up and configured. It is ready for you to use. Now that we have it set up with the right operating system and connected to the Wi-Fi, and we have it set up in a way that you can reach it remotely, it is time to learn some more about the different programming and codes that you can use to make sure that you get the most out of this device.

Chapter 3: A Look at How to Navigate Through the Menus, Folders, and Files of Raspberry Pi 3

Now that we have all of this already set and ready-to-go, it is time to learn some of the basics of going all the way through some of your menus, folders, and files using this device. There are a lot of these that can show up on this device, and knowing how to go through and make them work will make a difference in how much you are able to get done using the Raspberry Pi 3.

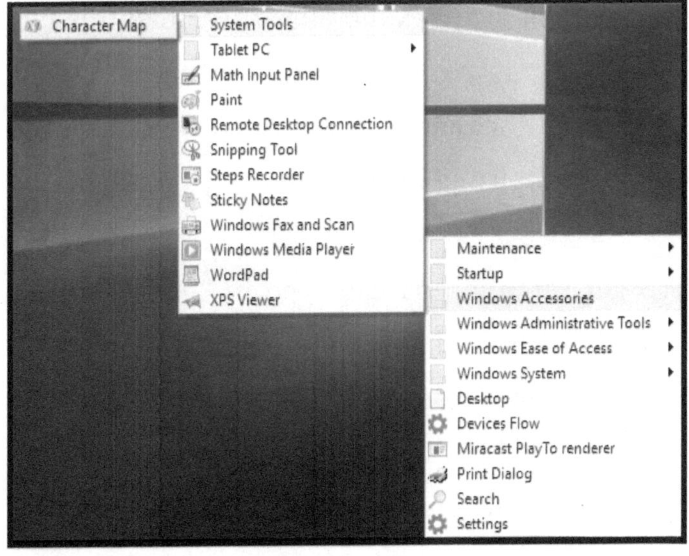

Source: Windows 10 folders [ONLINE]. Available at: https://i.stack.imgur.com/DjIY3.png [Accessed 30 March 2019]

Important Files

The first thing that we are going to look at is the files. If you would like to edit the files going from the command line, you can use the editor from Linux. There are a few options that you can choose from with these editors including Emacs, Vi, and Nano. For this chapter, we are going to take a look at the Nano editor. We like this one because it is really easy to use and it is the default editor that is installed, so we don't need to go through and do any extra steps to this.

To get this up, you can type in "*nano file.txt*", and then you will be able to edit the file that you want. Then press on CTRL + X to exit the program or the file when you are done. You can press the CTRL+O to save your file when you are done. To start though, we are going to use the command below in order to access the important files:

sudo nano /etc/wpa_supplicant/wpa_suplicant.conf

This is a file that is going to help us adjust the Wi-Fi connectivity that we have to the internet. You can then go through and enter in the SSID, or the name, of your network along with the password. Along with these parameters, you are able to enter in a lot of options to help you find what you want. For example, you can go through and enter whether the wireless network is hidden or not. Once this particular file is opened up, you will want to go through to the end of it, and make sure the following code is there:

```
network = [
        said="The_ESSID_from_earlier"
        ask="Your_wifi_password"
```

From this, you are able to change the default values that are there and get them to match the parameters of your network. You will need to use the "*sudo reboot*" command in order to restart the Raspberry Pi to make this work. You can go through and verify whether you were able to get this wireless network to hook up on your device by going to the command line and typing in "*ifconfig wlan0*". If filed "*inet addr*" has value, this means that the device was connected to the wireless successfully. If you find that there isn't value there, then it is time to double-check the parameters of the network again. You can use the code below to do this:

```
sudo nano /etc/default/keyboard
```

Now, one thing to notice here is that the keyboard of the Pi device may be in GB rather than US. This can cause some issues with the signs that you get. If you are using some of the codes that are needed here, make sure to take the time to change the keyboard layout from the GB over to US to ensure that you are able to get what you need.

Navigating the Menus in a Desktop Environment

When you are working with the operating system of Raspbian, you will find that the menus are not going to be that complicated. There is one of the big and main menus that you are able to reach, just by clicking on Raspberry, which you are able to find right at the top left corner of your screen. The main menu is going to consist of a few submenus with it such as preferences, help, accessories, games, internet, office, and programming.

The programming menu is going to consist of many different tools that can be useful for development on Raspberry Pi. You will be able to find the IDLE editor for Python 2 and 3. When you go to the submenu that is for office, you will be able to find the LibreOffice tools, and then there will be the submenu for the Internet, where you will be able to find all of the different browsers that you are able to access on your device.

There are many games that you are able to install on this kind of device, but you have to be careful with this because you want to make sure that you aren't going with games that take up a lot of space or need any special hardware with it. One of the games that you will notice that comes with the Raspbian operating system is the PI Minecraft. This is a special version of Minecraft that has been specially formatted and optimized to work with this device.

You can then move over to the submenu that is for accessories. This is a place where you can find a lot of different tools, such as the on-screen keyboard and so much more. Then we move to the submenu for the help, and you will be able to find a lot of the information that you need to help you work with a lot of the different parts of this device. You may find things like resources, guides, and instruction manuals for working with Raspberry Pi 3.

Next is the Preferences submenu. This is going to be where you are able to make some changes to the device to make sure that it is set up the way that you would like. This one is going to provide you with the configuration of this device. From this window, you are able to change the name of the device, pick out how you would like to boot the device (either from the command line or the desktop), change your password, do auto login, and even enable SSH to name a few.

As you can see, there are a lot of different things that you can do when it comes to working with the Raspberry Pi 3 device. Being able to access all of these different parts, and understanding what parts are already present inside the device is going to ensure that you are able to get the most out of this device as possible!

Chapter 4: Using the IDLE Editor to Write Your Own Python Programs

While some people like to work with the Raspbian operating system, you may find that as a beginner it is easier to work with the Python coding language. This coding language is super easy to work with, especially if you are someone who has never done any coding at all. There are a lot of reasons to love working with the Python language, and it often has a lot of power to ensure that you are able to create some of the different programs that you are looking at. However, before you are able to write any programs using the Python language, we first need to make sure that we have the IDLE editor in place. This chapter will show you exactly how to get this done.

```
Python 3.3.2 Shell
File Edit Shell Debug Options Windows Help
Python 3.3.2 (v3.3.2:d047928ae3f6, May 16 2013, 00:03:43) [MSC v.1600 32 bit (Intel)]
on win32
Type "copyright", "credits" or "license()" for more information.
>>> d = {"a":"apple","b":"boy","c":"cat"}
>>> d
{'a': 'apple', 'b': 'boy', 'c': 'cat'}
>>> t = ((k,v) for k,v in d.items())
>>> t
<generator object <genexpr> at 0x0237C558>
>>> for i in t: print(i)

('a', 'apple')
('b', 'boy')
('c', 'cat')
>>> for i in t: print(type(i))

>>>
Ln: 16 Col: 4
```

Source: Python IDLE [ONLINE]. Available at: http://i.stack.imgur.com/bz1qE.jpg [Accessed 30 March 2019]

The first thing that we need to do to start using the IDLE editor is to download it and install it. This is a program that you are able to download straight from the Python website at https://python.org/downloads. IDLE is going to stand for Integrated Development and Learning Environment, and when you get it from Python, it ensures that you have the right environment installed in order to write out the Python code, whether you are on Raspberry Pi or another computer.

There are a lot of things that you are going to enjoy when it comes to using the IDLE editor to write out some of your Python codes. Some of the features that come with this particular IDLE include:

Use the Tkinter GUI toolkit in order code in pure Python.

It is able to work on many platforms. This IDLE is set up to work on Mac OS X, Unix, and Windows, and it is going to work and look pretty much the same.

It includes the Python shell window, which is the interactive interpreter, with colorizing of error, output, and input messages in the code.

There is also a multi-window text editor that has a lot of features that you will find helpful when you are working on your code. Some of the features that you are able to use with this include auto-completion, call tips, smart indent, Python colorizing, and multiple undo.

You are able to search inside any window, search through more than one file, and replace things inside the editor window.

There is also a debugger in this IDLE that has persistent breakpoints, stepping, and viewing of both the local and the global namespaces.

It includes browsers, configuration, and other dialogs.

Once you are on the page to download the IDLE, you are able to choose which version of Python you would like to use. Right now you will want to work with either Python 2 or Python 3. The difference between these two versions is going to be very small, except that there is no more support and active development when it comes to Python 2.

In most cases, it is best to work with Python 3. However, there are a few instances when you would want to bring out Python2. One instance is if you are working with a machine on which the programming that is already there is carried out with the Python2 there. Another instance is if you are wanting to work with a specific utility or package from a third party that hasn't been able to release a version that is going to work on Python 3. In this tutorial, we are going to focus on just using Python 3 for all of the codings.

After you have gone through to the download page and clicked to get it on your system, give it a few minutes to install. You can run the IDLE by finding it in your application menu. Once it is running, there are going to be two main ways that you can write out the programs in your editor. You can choose to write the code right into the console—or you can open up a new document, write out the entire program, save it, and then when you are ready, you can run the code.

Both of these methods have been used by professionals and beginners alike, and often it is going to depend on the method that you like the best. In the next section, we are going to take some time to look at the examples of both of these and see which one is best for your needs. In most cases, if you are looking for a way to test out a piece of code, or if the program you want to work with is really small, then you would take the time to write it directly into the console. But if you are working with a lot of code and you don't want to have it get ruined, then it is best to do the second method.

The Process of Writing the Code Directly into the Console

When we are ready to write our code into the console, you will need to make sure that the code is entered in row by row. Then, when you are done with the row, you will need to press the Enter button so that you can go down to the next line. When you take the time to type in the keyword of "*def*" to your code, the program is going to recognize that what you want to do here is write out a function.

Once you have gone and entered the function, each click of the ENTER button is going to bring the typing console over to the next line. When you want to finish out that function, you would just write in "*return*". After you are out of the function with that command, you will simply be able to call it passing string argument. An example of the things that we have just talked about are below:

```
>>>def printString(text):
        print (text):
        return

>>>printString("Hello World"):
Hello World
>>>
```

When you go through and type this into your editor, you are going to get the result of Hello World to show up on your screen. We are going to spend some time talking about functions a bit more in the next chapter, but this is a good introduction to help you get started.

The Process of Writing the Code to a Document

When we are looking to write the Python program into a document so that we can save the different parts, it is necessary that we take a moment to be inside the editor and then choose in the top left corner "File" and then click on New File for your next option. When you click on this, you should have a popup of a new window.

From here, the first thing that we need to work on is to save the file that we want to work with. You can either choose to click on the file and then Save or just use the command CTRL+S. After you have been able to save the file, you can paste the code that we used in the previous example into the new file. When the code is ready, you can run it by simply pressing the Run option, and then clicking on either F5 or Run Model.

One thing to note here is that if your file isn't saved, the program is going to prompt us to save it. Once you decide to run the code, it is going to be executed in the Python Shell or the main window.

As you can see, both of these are pretty simple. The second option is usually best if you are working with longer pieces of code because it allows you the option to save the work as you go, and ensures that if something goes wrong with the computer, you aren't going to end up with a lot of lost work in the process.

Writing Comments in Python

The next thing that we need to take a look at in the Python language is the comments. There are going to be some times when you are writing codes, and you need to put in a little note about that particular part of the code. You may want to name the code, explain what you are doing at a certain part, or leave some other message or note to yourself inside the code. But you don't want the editor actually to go through and read that comment.

In order to write out some comments in Python and make sure that the editor isn't going to try to execute them, you need to use the hash character (or the # character) and extend to the end of the line. These comments can appear at the beginning of the line, or you can add them at the end when the code is all done. These comments are there in order to clarify the code, and the Python program isn't going to interpret them at all.

Basically, when you add in these comments, you will find that they won't change your output at all in the code, because the editor isn't going to look at it at all. But these comments are there to clarify the information and the output that is there.

There may be a few times when you will have a comment—or something that needs to be explained—and it is going to take up more than one line. If you do run into this problem, you are able to work with a multiline comment. These kinds of comments are going to start and then end with some triple quotes. This lets the editor know that you are writing out a long comment, and it will know when that comment ends so that it can go back to reading the code again.

Chapter 5: Some Basics of Writing the Python Code

We spent a little bit of time talking about how to work with the Python code above, but we need to go a bit more in-depth with this to ensure that we get this all set up in the proper manner. There are a few things that you will need to know in order to get the Python code to work in the proper manner for your needs and to make sure that you are able to create some of the codes on this device. While the Raspberry Pi 3 device does work with a lot of different types of programming languages, many beginners like to focus on the Python language because it is simple and easy to work with, and they can learn it even as a complete beginner to the coding world. Let's take a look at some of the basics of Python programming and how to write some of your Python code.

Regular Expressions

When you are working in the Python language, one thing that you will need to focus on is working with regular expressions—and these are going to bring you into the world of the Python library. You will be able to use these regular expressions are going to be used in your coding to make sure that you are able to filter out the different texts. It is possible for you to write out some code and then check to see whether that string or that text is found inside the code and to see if it matches up with your regular expression as well. Once you are able to do this inside the Python coding language, you will be well on your way to using it with other coding languages as well.

Thus, what are regular expressions, and how are you going to learn how to make them work inside of the codes that you want to write? A good place to start when it comes to regular expressions is to bring out your text editor and then find if there is a word that has been spelled in two different ways in the code. We are going to help you do a few things with the use of regular expressions so that this problem of misspellings won't cause as big of a problem as they could.

Let's take a look at some of the different things that you are able to do when it comes to regular expressions in your code.

Basic Patterns

One thing that you are going to like about regular expressions is that you won't be stuck just using them for specific fixed characters. They can also help you to watch out for some patterns if you need them to. Some of the patterns that are common with regular expressions include:

a, X, 9, < – ordinary characters just match themselves exactly. The meta-characters that aren't going to match themselves simply because they have a special meaning include: . ^ $ * ? { [] and more.

. (the period) – this is going to match any single except the new line symbol of "\n".

\w – this is the lowercase w that is going to match the "word" character. This can be a letter, a digit, or an underscore. Keep in mind that this is the mnemonic and that it is going to match a single word character rather than the whole word.

\b – this is the boundary between a non-word and a word.

\s – this is going to match a single white space

character including the form, form, tab, return, newline, and even space. If you do \S, you are talking about any character that is not a white space.

^ = start, $ = end – these are going to match to the end or the start of your string.

\t, \n, \r – these are going to stand for the tab, newline, and return.
\d – this is the decimal digit for all numbers between 0 and 9. Some of the older regex utilities will not support this so be careful when using it.

\ – this is going to inhibit how special the character is. If you use this if you are uncertain about whether the character has some special meaning or not to ensure that it is treated just like another character.

These are just a few of the regular expressions

that you can use when you work on your code. These are important to learn, so bring them out and place into your compiler to get some experience with them. There are a lot of codes when you are going to need them, and in some cases, you may need to use more than one to help you get the results that your code needs.

Doing the Queries in Python

One other thing that you are able to use these regular expressions within the Python language is to search, write, and match in the code. These are going to help you to change things inside the code that you are creating and can ensure that your edits are going to be in the right place.

The first method that we need to explore is the search method. This one is a good one to use any time that you want to make sure that your query is going to match up with something inside the code. Unlike some of the other methods that we will talk about, this one won't come with a ton of restrictions that you have to deal with. If you would like to have the search to go through the whole string, or just the end, or just the beginning–then the search is going to be the right one for.

The *search()* method is going to help you go through your string and see if something is there. Whether it happens in the front, middle or end of the string, the *search()* method is going to help you to find it. A good example of how you can work on this kind of method includes the following:

```
import re
string = 'apple, orange, mango, orange'
match = re.search(r'orange', string)
print(match.group(0))
```

Before we go any further, open up the compiler and type this code into it to see what output you are going to get. With this one, if you typed correctly, you are going to get the output of "orange" to show up on the computer. There could be one orange in the string, or there could be fifty—but this function is only going to give the output of one orange. You won't be able to see how many oranges are in the string; you will only be able to tell that orange appears somewhere in the string at least once.

The next option that you can go with is the match method. While there are many times that you can use the *search()* method to help you out, there are times when it won't be enough, and the *match()* method is going to help you out a bit more. This method is a bit better in some cases because it is going to find the matches that you need to your query, but this time, it is only going to tell you if that match happens at the beginning of the string. It will not look to see if there are matches later in the syntax or not.

Looking at the same example that we did above, you will see that there is a pattern of "*orange*" between all of the other words. But when you use the re_match method here instead of the search on, you will see that you don't get any results in the process. This is because it is only looking at the first term in the string to see if the orange is there with this one. Since the apple is listed first, this method will return no results.

And finally, the *findall* method is going to be a good option to use as well. If you look at the string above, you will notice that there are two oranges in the string, but neither of the two examples above shows you this. With the findall method, we are going to be able to see exactly how many of the same item is found in the string.

If you use the example above and put in findall, you will get the result of "*orange, orange*". This is going to be similar if there is only one orange in place or fifty oranges in place. The findall method is a good one to work with when you need to go through and figure out exactly how many of the item are found in that string, regardless of how many are there.

Loops

The next thing that we are going to learn about is the loops. These are going to be important to work with and can be similar to some of the conditional statements that you may have learned to use before. With these though, you are able to learn how to clean up the code a bit and can get a large amount of code written out in a short amount of time, without having to worry about the code looking like a mess.

The loops are going to be helpful any time that you are writing out a code where you would like the program to repeat something a certain number of times or repeat itself until some conditions are met, and you don't want to keep writing the same line out over and over again. If you need to make a multiplication table from one to ten, you don't want to go through and write out this line that many times. It can become tedious and can make the whole code look like a mess.

This may sound like a lot of work to focus on, but in reality, it is pretty simple to work with. And you will be able to get many lines of code written in just a few lines once you master this part of doing it all. The loop allows the program just to keep reading through the same part of the code over and over again until a new condition that you inserted has been met. You have to add this condition into the code, or you will freeze up the computer because it will just go in a continuous loop over again.

There are a few types of loops that you can work with. And the one that you choose is going to depend on what you are trying to do with the code. Each of them is going to work depending on the thing that you are trying to get done inside the code. The three loops that we are going to take a look at include the while loop, the for loop, and the nested loop.

The while Loop

The first type of loop that you can work within your Python code is known as the while loop. The while loop is the type that you will use if you want to make sure that the code goes through a cycle a predetermined number of times. You can set this number of times when you write the code to make sure the loop goes for as long as you would like.

With the while loop, your goal is not to make the code go through its cycle an indefinite amount of times, but you do want to make sure that it goes through for a specific number of times. If you are counting from one to ten, you want to make sure it goes through the loop ten times to be right. With this option, the loop is going to go through at least one time and then check to see if the conditions are met or not. So, it will put up the number one, then check its conditions and put up the number two, and so on until it sees where it is.

To give us a little bit better of an understanding on how these loops work, let's take a look at some sample codes of the while loop and see what happens:

```
counter = 1
while(counter <= 3):
        principal = int(input("Enter the principal
amount:"))
        numberofyears = int(input("Enter the
number of years:"))
        rateofinterest = float(input("Enter the
rate of interest:"))
```

```
        simpleinterest = principal *
numberofyears * rateofinterest/100
        print("Simple interest = %.2f"
%simpleinterest)
        #increase the counter by 1
        counter = counter + 1
        print("You have calculated simple interest
for 3 time!")
```

Now, open up the compiler and take some time to write this code out. Then see what information comes out when you execute with this code. You will see that when you are done writing this out, the output is going to come out in a way that the user is able to place any information in that they want. Then the program will take care of all the computations in order to figure out the interest rates, the final amounts, and so on based on the numbers that the user is able to place into the system.

You can choose how many times you would like the loop to go through its motions. We set this one up to go through the motions three times. What this means is that with this particular code, the user is able to put their results into the system three times, and then the system will either move on to the rest of the code, or end. You can always add in more or fewer loops depending on what works the best for your needs.

The for Loop

There are many times when you will want to work with the while loop that we talked about above. It is going to be strong enough and have enough power to help you get the results that you want with many of your codes. With that said, there are times when you need a loop, but the while loop is just not going to provide you with the results that you are looking for. This is when we are going to bring out the for loop. The for loop can be used in many situations, and in many coding circles, it is considered the traditional method of making loops.

When you are working with the for loop, you must set this up so that the user isn't the one who is able to provide information to the program. Instead, you will decide when the loop will stop. This allows you to have the loop go through the iteration, going in the exact order that you have set things up for. This information will then show up on the screen here, without the user having to input anything. An example of a code that can do this includes:

```
# Measure some strings:
words = [‘apple’, ‘mango’, ‘banana’, ‘orange’]
for w in words:
print(w, len(w))
```

When you work with the for loop example that is above, you are able to add it to your compiler and see what happens when it gets executed. When you do this, the four fruits that come out on your screen will show up in the exact order that you have them written out. If you would like to have them show up in a different order, you can do that, but then you need to go back to your code and rewrite them in the right order, or your chosen order. Once you have then written out in the syntax and they are ready to be executed in the code, you can't make any changes to them.

The Nested Loop

And now, it is time to take a look at the nested loop. This nested loop is a bit different than what we did with the other two loops above, but there are many programs that are going to use this to help them get more complicated processes done. When you do work with a nested loop, you will take one loop, and then place it inside of another loop. You will find that both of the loops are going to keep going over and over until they have reached their completion.

This may seem like something that is a bit strange to add into your code. Why would you want to have two loops working together and running at the same time? But there are actually many programs that you can work with and create that would need this to happen. For example, you could need to write out something like a multiplication table. You would like to have it fill itself in going from one all the way up to ten, and then the answers would be filled in to it.

If you had to go through and write out the code so that it did one times one is one, one times two is two, and so on until you got to ten times ten, this would take you forever and get tedious in the process. And it would really make the code look like a mess. It is fine if you choose to do this, but you can honestly use the nested loop and get the work done in just four lines of code, rather than the hundreds that it would take to use this in the traditional manner. The code that you need to make this happen and to create your own multiplication table includes:

```
#write a multiplication table from 1 to 10
For x in xrange(1, 11):
        For y in xrange(1, 11):
        Print '%d = %d' % (x, y, x*x)
```

When you got the output of this program, it is going to look similar to this:

1*1 = 1

1*2 = 2

1*3 = 3

1*4 = 4

All the way up to 1*10 = 2

Then, it would move on to do the table by twos such as this:

2*1 = 2

2*2 = 4

And so on until you end up with 10*10 = 100 as your final spot in the sequence.

Go ahead and put this into the compiler and see what happens. You will simply have four lines of code, and end up with a whole multiplication table that shows up on your program. Think of how many lines of code you would have to write out to get this table the traditional way that you did before? This table only took a few lines to accomplish, which shows how powerful and great the nested loop can be.

Working with Inheritances

While we are not going to spend much time writing codes that need inheritances in this guidebook, it is still a useful thing to know how to do in Python. This allows you to create a parent class and then bower it over and over again as you make each child class. This ensures that you are able to get the results and create a new class altogether.

When you are working with an inheritance, it means that you will take the original code that you are working on, and this one will be called the parent code, and then you can copy it down to come up with a new child code. This child code will start out being exactly the same as the parent code. But then the programmer can take that original code that is in the child code, and make any adjustments that are necessary to ensure that it works in the proper manner that they want.

As you work on the child code, you will notice that they are adjustable. This allows you to make any adjustments that you want, and any changes, without having to worry about how it will affect the parent code that you took it from. And there is the benefit of being able to just work with one leg of the inheritance, or you can keep on going and make a line of children codes.

This may sound like a complex thing to work with when you start to learn Python, but it is a simple code to learn considering all of the power that comes with it. You are able to add or take away or make any changes that you would like to ensure that the code, including the parent codes and the children codes, work the way that you would like. To help us get a good idea of what inheritance would look like when you are writing your own codes, take a look at the example below:

```
#Example of inheritance
#base class
class Student(object):
        def__init__(self, name, rollno):
        self.name = name
        self.rollno = rollno
#Graduate class inherits or derived from Student
class
class GraduateStudent(Student):
        def__init__(self, name, rollno, graduate):
        Student__init__(self, name, rollno)
        self.graduate = graduate

def DisplayGraduateStudent(self):
        print(”Student Name:”, self.name)
        print(“Student Rollno:”, self.rollno)
        print(“Study Group:”, self.graduate)
#Post Graduate class inherits from Student class
class PostGraduate(Student):
```

```
def__init__(self, name, rollno, postgrad):
Student__init__(self, name, rollno)
self.postgrad = postgrad

def DisplayPostGraduateStudent(self):
print("Student Name:", self.name)
print("Student Rollno:", self.rollno)
print("Study Group:", self.postgrad)

#instantiate from Graduate and PostGraduate
classes
objGradStudent =
GraduateStudent("Mainu", 1, "MS-
Mathematics")
objPostGradStudent =
PostGraduate("Shainu", 2, "MS-CS")
objPostGradStudent.DisplayPostGraduate
Student()
```

When you type this into your interpreter, you are going to get the results:

```
('Student Name:', 'Mainu')
('Student Rollno:', 1)
('Student Group:', 'MSC-Mathematics')
('Student Name:', 'Shainu')
('Student Rollno:', 2)
('Student Group:', 'MSC-CS')
```

You will find that these inheritances can add in a lot of freedom when it comes to what you can do while writing out a code. If you are working with the parent or the base class, and you would like to work on making a derived class out of it, you can use the idea of inheritance to get this done without having to go through and rewrite the code over again. Add in that you are able to keep and get rid of the exact features that you want, and you are able to create the exact derived classes that you want in Python.

Keep in mind that you can go through and create as many of these new derived classes as you would like. As long as you make sure that they go in order, and you use an example like what we wrote out above, you can keep on going down the line and making as many of these as you want. Just make sure that you keep them working off each other, going in a line, and doing a circular inheritance is not something that will work here.

These are just a few of the different topics that you may want to consider adding into your tool belt when learning a new language like Python. There are many more parts that can be just as important to ensure that you see some success with the codes that you want to create. If you are interested in really learning about the Python language and what it has to offer, you should take some time to learn about the Python generators, keywords, conditional statements, and more.

Chapter 6: Using the Raspberry Pi

Now that we have spent some time looking at the basics of the Python programming language, it is time for us to move on a bit and learn how to use the Raspberry Pi. Setting up the Pi to make sure that it works with the diodes, sensors, and other things that you want can sometimes be a challenge. However, we are going to spend some time talking about how to do all of this to ensure that you are set to go.

Ways to Interface the Electronics

The Raspberry Pi device is going to be useless if you are not able to use it in a way to interact and use other electronic devices. Here we are going to discuss how to get the Pi set up in a way that it works well with some of the other electronics that you want to use. This section is going to spend some time to discuss how to set up the Pi so that it works as well as it can with other electronics. First, you will need to have the proper equipment in order to make sure that you can make it work, and then destroy your circuit or even your Pi.

The first thing to look at is the multimeter—one that is digital. It is essential that you have one of these before you try to do anything with the circuitry of your device. This is a device that is able to measure a lot of different things that come with your device including the resistance, current, and voltage. This ensures that you won't accidentally start to pump the circuit and the device in a process with more than it can handle.

There are also a few discrete components that you need to learn how to work with. Some of these are going to include:

Diodes: This is going to be a semiconductor component that simply allows one current to flow in one direction, and ensures that this current is not allowed to flow the other direction.

Light emitting diodes or LEDs: This LED is going to act in a similar manner as a diode, just that it emits light of some color if the current flows in the right direction. There are many colors, sizes, and shapes for you to choose from with the LEDs. The length of the leg is going to determine which of the legs is positive and which one is negative.

Capacitors: A capacitor is going to be a component that can be used in order to store some of the electrical energy that you need. This can be useful when you want to store energy when there is a big difference in voltage between the two plates. Once the difference in voltage is able to dissipate, it is going to help to release the energy that is stored to ensure that it doesn't harm the Pi device.

Transistors: A transistor is going to be a semiconductor component that can be used to amplify or switch electricity or electric signals.

Optocouplers: These are helpful because they are going to be digital switching devices that ensure that you are able to isolate two electrical circuits from one another.

Switches and buttons: These are going to be pretty self-explanatory. These are going to be the input devices that you interact with to make sure that the circuit does something. Their basic function is to open or close a circuit. They will come in different shapes and forms, depending on what you would like to do with them.

The Communication Protocols

To make sure that your embedded system is able to work together well, there has to be some kind of communication between them. This is the way in which the data is transferred between the systems. There are certain standards that are going to be set in place to ensure that communication is coherent and consistent. These are going to be known as communication protocols.

There are a few different kinds of communication protocols that are in place, and the difference between them would be better understood if we learn a few concepts ahead of time. These important concepts are going to include:

Bitrate: This is going to describe the number of bits that are going to be sent per unit of time. This is going to be described in bits/sec.

Baud rate: While the bit rate spent time describing the number of bits sent per unit of time, the baud rate describes the number of symbols sent per unit of time. These symbols can each be of any number of bits. The number of bits is going to depend on the design. If the symbols are only one bit, the baud rate would then be equal to the bit rate.

Parallel communication: With this, you are going to see that there is more than one bit sent out at the same time.

Serial communication: With this kind of communication, the bits are going to be sent out in a way that has one at a time.

Synchronous serial communication: This is going to be a protocol of serial communication where the data that you need is sent at a steady and continuous stream at a very constant rate. This requires that the internal clocks of the two embedded systems be synchronized at the same rate so that the receiver gets the signal at the same intervals that the transmitter used.

Asynchronous serial communication: This form of serial communication doesn't require for you to have those internal clocks and synchronized. This data stream is going to contain start and stop signals before and after the transmission respectively. When the receiver gets the right start signal, it is going to prepare for the data stream that is coming. But when it receives the signal to stop, it is going to reset to the previous state so that it can be ready to receive a new stream later on.

Real-Time Interfacing Using Arduino

In case you are not familiar with it, Arduino is going to be a microcontroller that can be really powerful. You can use it along with the Raspberry Pi in order to make some really great projects. Of course, to make all of this to work, you need to get yourself an Arduino board. You will also need to have a good amount of programming expertise and mastery of interfaces to make it work as well. Of course, this is going to take more time than we have in this guidebook, so you can do some of your own research on this topic if you would like. With that said, there are a few key things that you can keep in mind with this including:

- You are able to interface with the Arduino using any of the other protocols of communication that we talked about above.

- You are able to configure the Arduino as an IC slave. This means that you are able to connect more than one Arduino to the device if you would like.

- A straightforward UART connection is only able to support one slave at a time so you may need to use a different kind of connection to get what you want.

If you would like to have an interaction that is high level and fast between the Pi device and the Arduino, then you will want to spend some time configuring your Arduino board as an SPI slave is the best way to go. This is due to the fact that the SPI connection will only be limited by the Arduino's clock speed.

Input and Output

When you look at the board of your Raspberry Pi board, you will notice that there are rows of pins that are on it. These are going to be the GPIO or General Purpose Input/Output. Using the software, you are able to designate whether each of these pins works for either input or output. And there are a lot of different things that you can do with these. Two of the pins are going to be 5V, and two more are going to be 3.3V. There are also a few ground pins that you are not able to configure at all. You can then use the rest as general purpose 3V2 pins.

Capturing Images, Audio, and Videos

It is possible to use the Raspberry Pi device in order to get audio, record videos, and capture photos. Of course, you are going to need to get a few peripherals if you want to make this happen. You will need to get a few items to make this happen, including the audio HAT, a USB audio, a Raspberry Pi Camera or a USB webcam.

Images and Videos

There are a lot of reasons why you would want to use your Pi device in order to capture all of the videos and images in the world around you. You can do it for video or image streaming, automation, robotics, and home security. If you have the right peripherals to work with, you can stream high-quality video. This stream, when it is done in the right manner, can be viewed asynchronously. The only limit that you are going to get to here is their duration, and that will depend on the capacity of the storage that you use.

To get started, you have to put a camera on. You

can either use a USB webcam or buy a camera that has been built to work specifically with the Pi device. We are going to discuss how to use the Raspberry Pi Camera option in order to shorten the explanation and to ensure that you are able to get it all done.

This camera is going to be tiny. It is going to attach to the Pi's camera serial interface or CSI with a ribbon cable. It isn't the best camera ever, but it is going to capture up to 5 megapixels and supports up to 1080p full HD video at several framerates, and you can sometimes go up to 90 frames per second on VGA resolution. You may also pick out a version that will allow you to get the infrared filter to help.

In order to get this special camera attached to the Pi device, there are a few steps that have to be taken including:

- Turn the device off. Make sure that you don't touch the metal contacts of your ribbon cable or you might ruin it.

- Take the lens protector off.

- Get the CSI connector and then gently pull up the housing clip. This is going to be either white or black.

- Insert the CSI cable into its slot.

Now you can push down the housing clip in order to let it get locked in place.

Now that this is in place, you can turn the Pi device pack on and configure the camera. You will be able to enable the camera with the following command:

```
pi@erpi ~ $ sudo raspi-config
```

Reboot the device.

If you would like to go through and capture images, you would need to input the following command:

```
pi@erpi ~ $ raspistill -o image.jpg
pi@erpi ~ $ ls -l image.jpg
```

This is just the basic of what you are able to do in order to get your system up and running. You can also do other things with this camera including setting up your own home security system or stream videos with this feature. There are so many great things that you are able to do with the webcam or camera, and you just need to take a few more steps to make it happen.

How to Record and Play Audio

Most of the time, when you are taking a video, you will want to make sure there is some audio or noise with it. And then there are times when you just need to have the audio. Sometimes you will want to connect a speaker to the Pi device to help you play music or make other noise. And we are going to take some time to make sure that you are able to get this audio up and running.

To get this audio set up, you need to have an audio input or output device. However, you will find that Pi devices are going to come with a built-in audio output system usually, and these will connect to the device with an HDMI port. For input, however, you will need to work with another device to help. Some of the options that you can use to make this happen includes:

USB audio: You are able to attach a USB audio input device to here as long as it is one that supports the Linux drivers. You may also use the USB webcams that we talked about before, just make sure that you choose one that has a microphone.

Bluetooth Audio: You can use either a Bluetooth audio input or an output system in order to connect back to the Pi device as long as you have a Bluetooth adaptor that is compatible with Linux.

Raspberry Pi HATs: HAT is going to be short for Hardware Attached on Top. You can choose to attach one of these in order to use all of the audio capabilities that come with the Pi device.

If you want to make sure that you can record and play any of the audio that is necessary on your device, you will need to make sure that you have the ALSA Utilities software. This is going to contain the *aplay* and the *arecord* utilities that you will need to record all of the audio that you need on this. To install this software to your device, you will just need to work with the code below:

```
pi@erpi ~ $ sudo apt update
pi@erpi ~ $ sudo apt install alsa-utils
```

And this should be enough to get it downloaded. You may need to go through and reboot the Pi device to make sure that it gets on the program the way that you would like.

Now, we need to take a quick look at how you can use this software, and the tools that come with it, in order to record and to play the audio that you need with either your own movies or with your music. To record the audio, you just need to use the following command:

```
pi@erpi ~/tmp $ arecord -f ed -D plughw:1,0 -d 10 test.wav
```

And then, when you are ready to make sure that the audio is going to play, you just need to work with the following command:

```
pi@erpi ~ /tmp # aplay -D plughw:1,0 test.wav
```

As you can see, there are a lot of different things that you are able to do when it comes to working with the Raspberry Pi product. We are going to take a look in this guidebook at some of the different projects and more that you are able to do with this device, and this section gave you some practice with the different coding and other things that you can learn how to do with this device to get the results that you want.

Chapter 7: How to Use GPIO Pins for Your Device

When you are taking a look at your Raspberry Pi 3, you will need to have some method that will allow you to interact with the outside world. This ability is going to come from the GPIO pins that are found in the board of your device. Since these pins are actually seen as the most important part of this device, there have been a lot of improvements that are done with these pins throughout the years. In fact, the latest version of Raspberry Pi 3 has 40 of these GPIO pins inside.

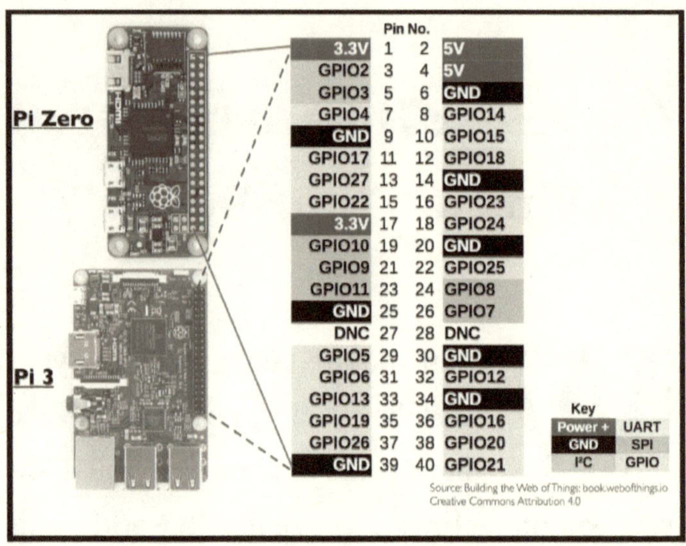

Source: GPIO Pins [ONLINE]. Available at: https://webofthings.org/wp-content/uploads/2016/10/pi-gpio.png [Accessed 30 March 2019]

One way to look at these pins is that they are seen as switches that have two states. These two states are going to be input and output. If we want to be able to read data off some of the sensors, such as using the computer to tell us the temperature, we are going to use the state of the input. However, if we would like to turn on some LED lights for our project, we would want to work with the state of the output.

When it comes to the GPIO pins on your device, there are going to be four colors represented, and these four colors are going to correspond to four types of pins. The red pins are going to represent the power, and they will usually have a strength somewhere between 3.3V to 5V depending on the device that you get. Then there are the black pins, which are going to be the grounds. These are going to be the output, and they will act like the negative terminal of your battery to help with some of the electricity.

Then we can move on to the yellow pins. These are the ones that you are able to program. Remember that we mentioned that there are two states with these pins, both the output and the input. When we work with the output, a pin is able to be set to either LOW (0) or HIGH (1), depending on whether we want to let them have power or not. When you are using the input, depending on the state of the output, we are going to read the 0 and 1 depending on the state of the sensor—and then there are the orange pins, which you will use if you wish to connect some additional boards along with the original one that you have.

An Example of How This Works

Let's say that we want to take our Raspberry Pi 3 and use it to control an LED light. In order to do this, you can use the following steps to make that happen:

- Connect the shorter wire of your LED light to the right resistor.

- Connect the other side of the resistor to GND pin on Raspberry Pi 3 Board.

Now you can connect the longer wire of LED Light to any of the yellow pins on the board.

And as you can see, this is a simple process. As

long as you know which pins you need to use, you will be able to make this all work well in order to get the results that you want. Once you get a bit of practice using these resistors and the pins, you will be able to get the projects to work, just by setting up the right pins with the right parts and the computer is able to get the results that you want.

Chapter 8: Tips and Tricks to Get the Most Out of Your Raspberry Pi

Now that we have spent some time talking about the Raspberry Pi 3 device and some of the neat things that you are able to do with it, it is time to take a look at some of the tips and tricks that you can follow to get the most out of this small computer. For each of the operating systems and for each device, there are going to be certain guidelines and rules that you need to follow and comply with when you use them. However, we are going to spend most of our time here looking at the shortcuts that are going to make your daily life with this device easier to work with. Some of the tips that you can follow when you want to get the most out of your Raspberry Pi 3 device include:

Download Chromium

If you want to be able to use your Raspberry Pi 3 to surf the web at all, then you are going to find that there are a lot of sites you will visit that what you to work with JavaScript. And when they do require this, the speeds to load the information can be incredibly slow. A good service to use is Chromium, and this is a decent alternative to Iceweasel and Epiphany when it comes to handling these sites.

Work with a Script Blocker

Another thing that you can do to make sure that you are able to bypass all of the hiccups and lag that occurs when you are online and surfing the web is to make sure that the loading of scripts is turned off. This isn't as hard to do as it may seem. You are able to do this by installing Mozilla's browser for Linux called Iceweasel. After you install this, you will then go to the add-on page for Mozilla, and then install the NoScript extension.

This is a nice extension to use because it is going to block the JavaScript across the web, which ensures that you are able to get much better speed when you are loading a new page. Of course, there is a big drawback to using this script, and that is that some, and often this is the essential part, of the page or content is not going to show up for you. This is because many times that content needs to have the JavaScript in order to work. If the JavaScript is turned off, then there is no way to get JavaScript to work.

It is up to you to determine what scripts you would like to show up on the page or not. You can go to the upper right corner of your screen and there you are going to notice an icon of this extension. You can click on that and choose the script that you would like to have loaded up afterward.

Try to Limit How Many Things Are Running at a Time

Remember that this is a small computer. It is not going to be able to handle all of the things that you are used to doing on a bigger computer. There is only 1 GB of RAM available on this device, and this means that your potential for going through and doing more than one task at a time is limited.

When you are using the Raspberry Pi 3, remember that you should avoid opening up two browsers at the same time, or more than four tabs in one browser. This is going to take up all of the space that is available on your system and can make it harder to get things done. Also, you need to be careful about opening browsers or any other heavy programs, like LibreOffice or similar because it is possible that the Pi device will get stuck.

Don't Worry About a Big Keyboard or Monitor

One mistake that a lot of beginners are going to make when they get started with the Raspberry Pi 3 is that they think to make it work they need to have a big keyboard and a big monitor. This is going to cause a lot of extra work for you as you try to carry all of those different items around, and the truth of the matter is that you don't even need them.

Many of the developers who are currently working with this device don't realize that there are actually some nice and compact touchscreens on the market available to use with the Raspberry Pi device, and made to ensure that life is as easy as possible. Taking the time to connect your monitor to the Pi device with an HDMI can be difficult when you are developing on the go, so having a dedicated screen can be a big life saver. There are also some smaller 2.8-inch screens that you can touch, and even some that are a bit bigger at 7 inches. You can pick the ones that work the best for you.

The touchscreen is not only the perfect size to go with your Raspberry Pi 3 device, and can make life easier there. But going with this can also solve your problem when it comes to needing a keyboard. If you just use a keyboard on occasion with the device, then the touchscreen will be plenty to take care of this and get the results that you want. However, if you are someone who likes to type in your commands and you spend time doing terminal work, then you may want to keep a keyboard around some of the time.

Remember that there are different options for keyboards that work specifically with the Raspberry Pi products. While some of the regular attachable keyboards can work, they are often really bulky and hard to work with and can take a lot of time and effort to take around with you. There are smaller versions that you can choose to work with depending on your needs.

Use the Raspberry Pi as a Virtual Assistant

Devices like Google Home and Amazon Echo are changing the way that we look at technology, and they are really helping to bring the idea of a personal virtual assistant t homes around the world. Those who are keen on using Raspberry Pi can also use it to create their own virtual assistant, for a lot less money. And you won't need to purchase the pre-built device because you can get the virtual assistant to work on the Pi device itself. As long as you are able to go through and write out a few codes in Python, you will be able to make this one work as your virtual assistant.

Flash Photography Could Reset the Pi

One thing that you may need to take a look at with the Pi device is that using it around flash photography could have the negative effect of resetting the PI. This is seen more in the Raspberry Pi 2 device and isn't as prevalent when we are taking a look at the Raspberry Pi 3, but it is still something to consider. If the camera flash is really bright or really close to the device, then it is going to make it more susceptible to the issue and can make all of the hard work that you already did on the product go away.

If you are going to be somewhere wherein flash

photography will be used a lot, or if you are going to use some sort of flash photography around the device, then you really need to be careful. You don't want to end up harming the device in any way and causing it to get damaged when you are working on a difficult project.

Try Out Some of the Projects

This guidebook has taken some time to go over a few of the projects that you are able to do when you work on the Raspberry Pi 3. There are a lot of other cool things that you can do with this product as well, and you can turn it into almost anything that you would like. All that it takes is some practice and the right code to make it all happen.

With that said, the only way that you are going to get better with what you are doing with this device is to get more and more practice. Make sure to try out all of the projects that are in this guidebook, and come up with a few on your own. This will ensure that you are able to really get your hands on the Pi device and see what it can do for you.

Learn a Coding Language

We have spent some time in this guidebook exploring the use of the Raspbian operating system and the Python coding language. These are two very good options to work with when you are trying to get the hang of your device, and many programmers choose to work with these. But there are a lot of other coding languages that you can choose to implement into this and see great results as well.

Whether you choose to work with the Python coding language or another type, make sure that you learn one to go along with this device. Being able to code some of your own programs, rather than just going around and hoping that you can get the results from someone else, will open up a lot of doors for you when creating some of your own projects.

Chapter 9: How to Install a Heat Sink

One of the features that you may want to add onto your Raspberry Pi 3 device is something known as a heat sink. In most cases, these are not going to be essential—but it can be nice if you use your Pi device on a regular basis and if you want to make sure that you don't get it overheated or run into some other problems with the device.

The heat sink is a nice addition because it helps to prevent some of the overheating that is common with the Raspberry Pi devices. But when you just use the most basic usage with this device and when you aren't trying to do any heavy lifting, you will find that this device is not going to generate a lot of heat. If you don't plan to do much more than just experiment a bit with the device and learn how to use it, then you will find that the components of the device aren't going to be under much risk whether you use the heat sink or not. It is up to you in this situation.

When you are using the most basic version of the Raspberry Pi 3, it is not going to come with a heat sink. This is further proof that even the manufacturer wasn't too considered that those with the basic usage of this device would need to use the heat sink. If you don't want to work with one, that is fine. But for some people, it is an added bonus. And for others, depending on what they plan to do with the device, it is a big necessity.

However, if you went through and purchased one of these devices and it came in the package with the heat sink, go ahead and install them. This is a very nice thing to add because it ensures that your product is going to have a bit more thermal protection than normal. Don't let the fear of thinking this process is too difficult to stop you from using this device in the right way. It is only going to take about five minutes to put on, and you will be able to handle the Raspberry Pi 3 device as intensely as you wish once the heat sink is placed on it.

For those who are just beginners, it is just a personal preference. But as you start learning more about the Raspberry Pi device, and you start using it for more and more things, then it is possible that the server can get overloaded and it may even start to overclock. Once these things start happening, it means that you will need to go through and monitor the temperature of your Raspberry Pi as closely as possible so that it doesn't get ruined.

We will take a look later on at some of the things that you can do to ensure that this device stays at the temperature that it should if you allow it to get too warm, and you allow it to stay at that elevated temperature for too long, then you are going to run into some troubles with how the system works. But before we get to that, let's take a look at some of the simple steps that you can use to install the heat sink on your Pi device.

The Process of Installing the Heat Sink

First, the heat sink needs to be installed on two components of the Pi device. These include the processor and the NIC, which you will find close to your USB ports. The bigger part of the heat sink is going to go to the CPU in the center. The other part is going to go into the LAN chip. The orientation of the heat sink doesn't matter. You just need to work to see if it will get centered on the CPU so that the heat is able to low over this surface as smoothly as possible. Some of the steps that you can work on in order to make sure that the first heat sink is placed onto the device in the proper manner include:

- Take the first heat sink, which is going to be the larger of the two.
- Look for the adhesive pad that is underneath this heat sink, then peel it off.
- Place the heat sink onto the right processor that we talked about above.
- Press down lightly to ensure that the heat sink is able to attach in the proper manner.

You can then repeat the above steps with the second heat sink, but make sure that this time it is going to be stuck on the NIC. You can then take the device in your hands and tighten up the heat sinks with your thumb and index finger in order to complete the operation. Once the heat sinks are all installed, it should start to look something like this:

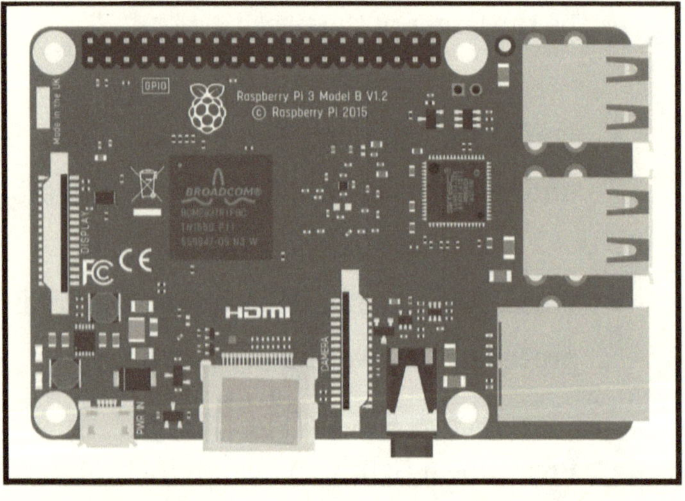

Source: Raspberry Pi 3 illustration [ONLINE]. Available at: https://commons.wikimedia.org/wiki/File:Raspberry_Pi_3_illustration.svg [Accessed 01 April 2019]

And that is all that you need to do to get it set up on your system. It is that easy, and as long as you know where to install the pieces, you are set to go.

Now that we have these all set up in the right spots, it is time to take a look at how you make sure that the Raspberry Pi doesn't get too hot, and that you are able to monitor the temperature as well as you can. You don't want to allow the Pi device to get too hot, or it is going to run into trouble working in the proper manner.

The first thing to look at is the maximum safe temperature. The lower you are able to keep the temperature of your CPU, the more efficient it will end up being. You will find that once this device gets to 85 degrees Celsius, it is going to really start to run slower. And once it gets to this temperature, it is time to turn the device off and give it time to cool down. If the temperature goes even higher, then you are risking a lot of CPU damage in the process.

So, how do you check to see what the temperature of the CPU is at any time? If you are on your Raspberry desktop, you should go through and add in the current temperature. This allows you to check the current temperature of the device at any time that you would like. The steps that you need to ensure that you can monitor the temperature by putting it onto the Raspberry desktop taskbar includes:

- Click right on the taskbar.
- Then click on the add/remove panel items button.
- From here, click on the Add button that will show up in the right menu.
- From the list that you receive, choose the temperature monitor that is there.
- Click Add.

The top bar should not let you see what the current temperature of the CPU is. You are able to customize the order of the items on the taskbar any time that you would like, and you can add space between the elements.

Another method that you can use is to do this with the command line. If you want to, you can type in the command and ask it to tell you the right temperature at any time that you want. The command that you will need to work with to make this happen includes:

```
/opt/vc/bin/vcgencmd measure_temp
```

What if the temperature is too high?

If you installed some heat sinks and have watched the temperature to try and keep it down, but you still find that the CPU is coming in at a level that is too high, then it is time to put in some work to improve the way the device is able to cool down. Some of the ideas that you are able to use to make this happen includes:

- Check out the environment that is around you, then ensure that this is not the reason that the temperature of your device is getting worse. For example, if the device is under direct sunlight, or you have it right next to the radiator, that may be part of the problem.

- Take a look at the device and see if there is any dust present that is clogging up the components.

- Think about investing in better equipment such as water cooling stuff, fans, a better case with more ventilation, and bigger heat sinks.

And that is what you need to know to work with

heat sinks. These are a great device to add to your product if you are worried that the work you are doing is going to run the device and make it not perform the way that you want. These heat sinks will help to keep the temperature of the device at a comfortable level so that you can keep using the Raspberry Pi 3 device, without worrying that the parts are going to be damaged in the process.

Chapter 10: How to Create Your Own Arcade Box

One of the first projects we are going to explore in this guidebook will be the arcade box. This may seem like a more complicated project to work with, but it is a great way to get things started and will give you some practice and some idea on how the arcade box works.

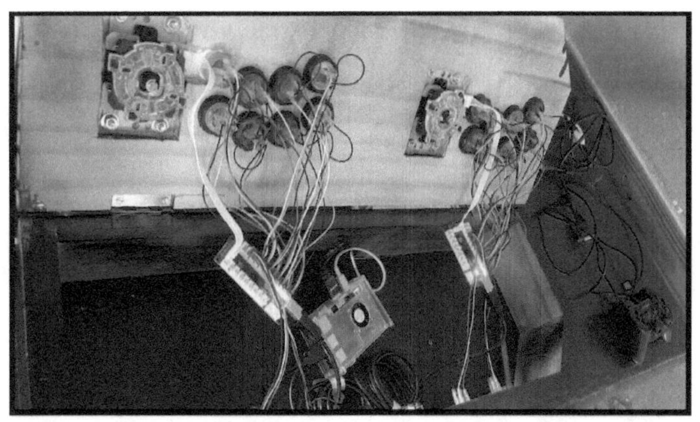

Source: Raspberry Arcade Box [ONLINE]. Available at: https://commons.wikimedia.org/wiki/File:Arcade_por_dentro.jpg [Accessed 01 April 2019]

The previous chapters that are in this guidebook have spent time exploring a few aspects that are more technical of working with the Raspberry Pi 3. Now it is time to put some of this new knowledge to the test with a few sample projects. These are the ones that you can try out to make sure that you learn some projects, and the arcade game is a good way to make this happen.

The Raspberry Pi 3 is a great device to work on with the arcade box because it can hold a lot of different games on it, especially if you are working with some SD cards to hold some of the games. But the first step that we need to use to make this happen is to make sure that we have all of the accessories and tools in place. Some of the supplies that are important for working with this project will include:

- A game controller is not necessary, but it can make playing some of the games a little bit easier.

- A power supply so that the device turns on.

- The Raspberry Pi 3 (or other Raspberry Pi device that you want to use).

- A good SD card (This card needs to be at least 4GB in order to make the games work).

- An HDMI cable to hook your device up to a monitor.

- A TV.

The first step is to get the games from the RetroPie website over to your PI. We are going with the RetroPie website to help us get some of the older games that we are going to use for this device. You will simply need to download the website over to your SD card so that it can then be put on the Pi device.

To do this, visit retropie.org.uk/download, and from there, you are able to pick out the version of the Raspberry device that you want to work with. Give it some time to copy over to your SD card.

Once everything is over on the SD card, you can turn on the Raspberry device. Add in the controller and plug the device into the television while you wait for it to load up. Add the SD card inside the device and give it a few minutes to boot up. If you did the conversion properly, then you should see the EmulationStation come up on the television screen.

As you get to this step, and that part is showing on the screen, you are able to go through and make sure that any of the configurations that are needed here get done. The controller is often a better thing to use because it makes it easier. And with the controller, you can just go through and click on the things as needed to finish it up and get everything set up the way that you want. Remember that the first time you go through and do all of this is going to take a bit longer than the other times because it needs to be downloaded a bit and handled. Once everything is saved in there the right way, you will find that the process gets a lot easier—when you are all done with the setup up, double-check that you saved the work to ensure that it doesn't get lost and that you won't have to go through and do it all over again.

Another thing to check here is to make sure that you have the Wi-I already set up and working on your device. We talked about how to do this earlier, and if you already took those steps, then you won't have to go through and do them again here. If you haven't, then now is the time to get it done to ensures that you can actually play the games.

After your Wi-Fi is hooked up to the Raspberry Pi 3 device and you are certain that it is on and running, you will then need to take a few minutes to add the ROMS to this device, and getting them moved over can take a few minutes. This process is pretty simple and works similar to what we did before, but you either need to work with an Ethernet cord or make sure that your internet connection is as strong as possible.

If you don't have a strong internet connection, and the ROMS gets interrupted in the process, then you are going to run into some trouble. It is your choice whether you would like to do a test on your internet to see if it is steady and strong enough, but often it is better to work with the Ethernet cord to be safe.

Go onto your main computer. If you are using a Windows computer, you can open up into the file manager on the computer and type in a simple code of "*//retropie*". If you are working with a Mac computer, you can go to the finder on the computer, select on Go, and then click on Connect to Server. You would then type in the code "*smb://retropie*". Both of these end up with the same results—they just have to be done a bit differently on different computers.

Once you have the Wi-Fi and everything connected properly, you can then work on the

ROMS over to your Raspberry Pi device. We need to do this remotely so your choices are to use an SD card to move all of the games over or you can pick and choose which of the games are the most important to you to move over. Once they are transferred over through the SD card, you can begin playing your new arcade box.

And that is all that you need to do to get the Raspberry Pi 3 set up on your computer as an arcade game. You will be able to add in any of the games that you want at this point. There are a lot of options to choose from too! If you are only planning on downloading a few of these to start, then it is fine to put them directly on the Pi device.

But if you are someone who is an avid gamer, and who wants to be able to access a lot of games at any time, then this is going to fill up the device very quickly. It is much better to put the games on SD cards to hold them, and just switch these in and out whenever you want to play them. This ensures that you are able to get the results that you want, without taking up too much space on the device.

Chapter 11: Can I Turn My Raspberry Pi 3 into a Phone?

The next project that we are going to take a look at is turning the Raspberry Pi 3 into your own phone. While this kind of phone may not be as high-tech as you will find with some of the smartphones and other products that are out on the market, the fact that it only takes a few steps in order to turn this simple computer into a simple phone that you can use for some basic functions like calling is pretty amazing.

Source: Raspberry Phone [ONLINE]. Available at: https://en.wikipedia.org/wiki/File:Raspberry-Pi-Zero-FL.jpg [Accessed 01 April 2019]

If you are looking for another project to work on, and you have been curious to find out if you are able to make your own phone, without having to spend a ton of money each month to a phone company all the time, then this is the project that is going to work the best for you. For this one, we are going to take the basic Raspberry Pi 3 device and use it in order to make our very own phone. And the neat thing is that we just need to work with a handful of supplies to do it. Even though this sounds like a really complicated project to get started with, it is pretty simple, and it won't be long until you are able to get your phone up and running and ready-to-go. Some of the things that you will need to get started with turning the Raspberry Pi 3 into a phone includes:

- Headphones
- Microphone
- An electrical switch
- Velcro squares to help hook it all together
- A touch screen
- GSM module that has an antenna and some audio outlets
- Battery pack to help power the phone
- A Raspberry Pi 3 that can handle the Python coding language
- Duct tape
- Cables
- Zip ties
- A sim card

- A converter for DC-DC
- A foam board that you are able to cut down to be the same size as the Raspberry Pi

When you are picking out the supplies that you need for this project, you should double-check that they are going to be compatible with the Pi 3 and not one of the other versions of Raspberry Pi. There are a lot of choices out there in terms of the supplies that you can use, and many of them come in at a lower price. But you want to make sure that they are of high enough quality, and that they are actually going to work with the device that you want to use.

Once you are sure that all of the supplies that you have are compatible with the device, it is time to make sure that the right software is on the device. For this one, you will need to work with the Python coding language a bit, so make sure that the Pi device has this language added to it. While you are at it, you will also need to have the WireHunt and the PiPhone software added to the device so that it is going to turn the computer into the phone as we want. You can also move these pieces of software over to your device with the help of an SD card to help get it all started.

Now that we have all of these items present, it is time to get started to turning this computer into a phone. The first step to doing all of this is to connect the battery. You need to do this over the switch so that the battery has the right amount of power that it needs. Once this is done, you can hook both of these to the GSM module. Take the header of the GSM and connect it back to the converter that you are going to use.

Once you have had a chance to connect all of these, it is time to hook them up with your chosen Pi device. You can use this with the other cables that you have. Next, connect the device with the rest of the transmit pins so that everything stays together. Check that the pins are connected to the Rx and T ports. While this does include a lot of connecting, once all of this is connected, it is time to take the SIM card and connect it.

Now that all of those lines are connected and the SIMs card is in place, it is time to assemble all of the parts. To make sure that this works, you will need to take the piece of foam that was on the list and cut it down until it is the same size as your Raspberry Pi. Place the Pi device over it and use the Velcro squares, and a bit of duct tape. This will help you to connect the switch, module, and converter to the other side of the foam. You want to make sure that you put the battery pack in a secure place, somewhere between the screen and the Pi device. You don't want the battery pack to move around and cause troubles, or the phone won't work the way that you want.

If you took the time to connect all of the parts properly, you would notice that the phone is pretty much done, and you will be able to use it properly. At this point, you just need to turn on the switch with the phone to get it to work. From here, you are able to dial in any number that you would like to use on the phone and make a call.

This is a simple phone, so you won't be able to go through and do a ton of things on it. But it will allow you to make and receive calls. There are projects that help you to get more out of the phone if you would like, and will make it easier to turn this into a better phone, but for a beginner, you now have a simple phone to work with that takes and receives calls.

Chapter 12: Turning the Raspberry Pi into a Media Server

The next project that we are going to take a look at is how we can turn the Raspberry Pi 3 into our own personal media device or media server. You will find that this can be an incredibly useful thing to work with—and even though it sounds pretty complex, there are really only a few steps that you have to take to make it happen.

This project is a great idea to work with if you are interested in making a media server, whether you would like to use it on your own or you want to make it strong enough that others inside your home are able to work with it at the same time as you do. You will find that it is even possible for you to go through this project and make the changes necessary so that only certain people can come and use the device.

There are a few tools that you need to have in place before you are able to start turning the Raspberry Pi 3 device into your own media server. You will need the Raspberry Pi 3 device, of course, a really strong connection to the internet or an Ethernet cord, and an SD card that is able to hold a minimum of 8 GB—but you may find that you need a bit more as well.

As we start this project, we are going to make the assumption that you already have the Raspbian operating system added to your device to speed this along. Once you have that operating system in place, the steps that you can take to start turning your Raspberry Pi into a media device include:

Check out the device you are using and check to see if it is updated. If you just purchased the Pi device, then this shouldn't be an issue. But if you have had it for some time, then type in the code "*sudo apt-get update*". This will show you if there are some updates and then you can let the device go from there.

Once the system has time to get all the updates, you can move over the HTTPS transport package. You must add this on because it will use the packages that you need for this media service. To get this, you just use the "*apt-get*" command inside your code. So, to make the HTTPS package show up, you would type in "*sudo apt-getinstall apt-transport-https*".

After that code is done, you will need to go through and make sure that there is a crypt key that you can add to the:

sudo tee/etc/apt/sources.list.d/pms.list

When we get to this point, you can go through and look through the list that comes with the package. You want to make sure that it is up to date the way that it should be. You can use the following code to check for this:

```
sudo apt-get update
```

While you are going through these steps, if you see that there is an error, this most likely is that the transport package wasn't able to go through and be installed properly. Make sure to double-check this and if it wasn't done the right way, then go through the steps above again before moving on.

Once you are sure the package is on the right way, then you need to do the following installation to get your plex media server installed on the device:

```
sudo apt-get install -t Jessie plexmediaserver
```

If an error ends up on the screen with this step, you need to do some troubleshooting here. This can take some time, but it is usually something pretty simple to get the plex media to work the way that you want.

You need to make sure that you don't run into issues with copyright and permissions here. To do this, you need to use a code to make sure that the plex is running with the user of the Pi device. The code for this is:

```
sudo nano/etc/default/plexmediaserver
```

If you would like to change the name of your user from plex to Pi, just use the following code:

```
PLEX_MEDIA_SERVER_USER=pi
```

Now you will need to take some time to restart the media server for plex. You will be able to do this with the following command:

sudo service plexmediaserver restart

At this point, the program should be installed to the Pi, but keep in mind that you need to check that the IP that is on the Pi is static so that it is easier to remember this IP address when you need it later. To figure out what the current IP address is, type in the following:

Hostname -I

Now you can open up the cmdline.txt file to make some changes. Just type in sudo nano /boot/cmdline.txt

At the bottom of the file, you will be able to replace the YOUR IP with the IP address that came from your hostname -I command. To do this, just type in ip=YOURIP.

Here you should exit out of your program, making sure to save it as you leave.

By this point, it is a good idea to do a reboot with the sudo command so that the Pi program is sure to have the IP address that you want to use with it. Once the reboot is done, double-check the IP address to see if it made the right changes.

Ways to Store the Media

Now that we have spent some time talking about how to turn your device into a media center, it is time to actually learn the steps that you need to store media on that device so you can pull it out to use later. With the steps that we listed above, the device is ready to use, but there aren't any media found on it. You have to go through and do that in order to get the most out of it.

One way to add on the media that you would like to use and hear with the Raspberry Pi device is to bring out the external hard drive and use a cable to hook it up with the Raspberry Pi. You can then move the movies, music, and other media that you would like over to the Pi device, and listen and enjoy any of the media that you choose.

Another option to work with is to take the device after it is done being configured, and then plug it into whatever hardware or device is holding onto your chosen media. Let's say that the media is found on your desktop or personal computer. You would simply need to take the Pi device and plug it into your regular computer, or some other device, and then transfer the media right over. You can then just make sure that you have access to the Plex software, and then take the time to download all of the media that you would like to transfer over before you are able to use it on the Pi device.

A third option that is available is to work with your own personal SD card to move the media over where you would like it. You can take the SD card and place it into your computer, or another device that holds the media, and then move all of the music, movies, and other media onto the card. Once the media is all transferred over, you will then be able to put the SD card into the Raspberry Pi media player and listen and enjoy the media at any time that you would like.

This method can be nice because it is going to ensure that everything is going to stay in one place, and there won't be any worries about whether the memory on the Pi device is going to have enough room to hold onto the media that you would like to use. You can hold as much media as you want because you can just keep filling up SD cards and switching them around depending on the one that you would like to listen to.

As you can see, making your own media player out of the Raspberry Pi device isn't as complicated as it may seem. You will have to take some time to go through the 15 steps that are above, and you will need to write out some code. But considering you are taking a basic computer and turning it into the media device that you can use all the time, it is fairly easy and straightforward to work with. The Raspbian operating system ensures that you are able to get this done pretty quickly, and helps you to get to listening to all of your favorite media in no time at all.

Chapter 13: The Best Accessories for Raspberry Pi 3 to Make It Work Better

There are a lot of different options that you are able to do when you are working with the Raspberry Pi 3 computer on its own. You can do a lot of the projects that we talked about above without needing to go through and get a lot of accessories in this device. However, if you would like to get your Pi device to do even more than it can on its own, then it could be really helpful for you to have a few accessories on hand as well.

There are actually quite a few accessories for you to use with the Raspberry Pi. This chapter is going to take some time to list out some of these accessories and describe these in detail. With the advent of Raspberry Pi 3, demand for accessories such as Bluetooth adapters and Wi-Fi adapters significantly decrease. In addition to the one-piece accessories, there are accessories kits—a few of them we will mention below.

Breadboard

The first accessory that you are able to use with your Raspberry Pi 3 is the Breadboard. This is going to be an essential component of any project that you are going to work on with this device. This is a good thing to use when you want to prototype your circuits. Using this particular component, we are able to easily plug in or out the different actuators or sensors without the need for soldering.

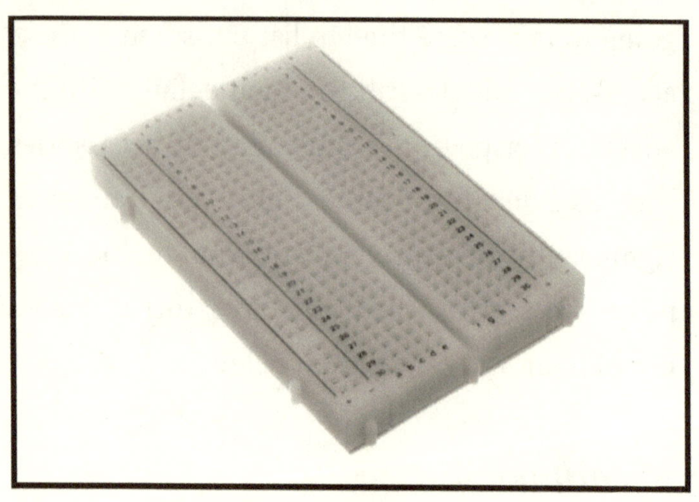

Source: Breadboard [ONLINE]. Available at: https://commons.wikimedia.org/wiki/File:400_points_breadboard.jpg [Accessed 02 April 2019]

When you are looking at a breadboard, there are going to be a lot of holes in it, and each of them is going to be spaced about 0.1 inch apart. There are a few different variations of the breadboard. Some of these are going to come in one section, but often they are going to be made with the use of two sections. Sometimes the boards that have two sections have a small bridge in the center that will go from one side over to another, and it can help you to divide up one section from another. Also, on each section, you will notice that there are two rows that are pretty long, and these are going to be designed to provide easy access to the power and to the ground. These are going to be known as power rails.

Make sure that you find the right breadboard for your needs. There are a few different types that we just talked about, so, you need to make sure that you go with the one that is the best for your project needs.

The Raspberry Pi Heat Sink

Another thing that you can consider using with your Raspberry Pi 3 is going to be the Heat Sinks. This one is helpful because you are able to add it to the device to ensure that it stays cool and that you don't have to worry about your device getting too hot. These Heat Sinks are going to come with a thermal layer that is adhesive, and they will be made out of aluminum.

You will also notice that these can help to reduce the risk that you face of hardware failure. Heat sinks are going to be pretty small. But this allows them to fit in with all of the types of Raspberry cases that are out there. There are also going to be several sizes that are available depending on which components you would like to have cool down, such as the GPU and the CPU.

The Raspberry Pi Camera Module

There are actually two versions that come with the Raspberry Pi camera. The latest version is V2. This can be useful if you would like to take pictures as well as an HF video. It is going to be easy for a lot of beginners to work with, but it is also going to provide you with a ton of possibilities as a developer who is more experienced.

When you compare this to the first version that came out with this camera that only came with the lens being 5 megapixels, this version is going to be improved in several ways, including a lens that is 8 megapixels. It is going to support a few video modes including VGA90, 270p60, and 1080p30. The camera is also going to come with a 15cm cable.

You can see on the official website that they discuss how the cable length should not be changed because it is going to affect the quality of the camera. However, if you are an enthusiast with this kind of product and you know what you are doing, there are a lot of enthusiasts who like to work with this kind of camera and change it to an HDMI adapter. When you are able to work with these adapters, you will find that the HDMI cable is able to extend how much distance you can get between the camera and your device.

The Raspberry Pi Case

You may find that having a case for the Raspberry Pi 3 can be really useful, especially if you plan to transport it on a regular basis. On the one hand, there are going to be a few advantages, such as making sure that the device is protected in case something happens. When you travel with this device, you will find that there is a lot of potential for accidents to occur. Having the case available will help to make sure that the computer stills works.

However, there is a disadvantage of working with this as well. For example, if you have a case on the device, then you will have trouble gaining access to the pins, and it is harder to do the work that you want without taking the case off. And if the device is inside a case, it is going to take up more space than just being on its own.

There is an official case that is available for this device, but, if you don't like that case or would like to find something that is a little more unique and more your style, you are able to find a lot of non-original cases to work with. Even if you do decide to make a case for yourself, but you need to pay attention to the places where the cables come in, and the cooling of the device. According to the official of the Raspberry Pi website their case has the following features:

- High-quality ABS construction.
- Light pipes for power and activity LEDs.
- Removable side panels and lid to make sure that you are able to access the display connectors, camera, and GPIO easily.

Raspberry Pi Displays

There are many different types of displays that you are able to use with this device. One example of this is the monochrome LCD displays, with one or more lines, small touch screens, and even larger touch screens that are seven inches or more. Many people like to work with the touch screen options because it allows them to turn this into an all in one device.

There is an official seven-inch touch screen that you are able to get from Raspberry Pi. This is going to connect to the device through the adapter board that is responsible for signal conversion and for handling power, and the resolution on the screen is going to be 800 by 480. However, you are able to go through and pick out a different screen if you choose.

The nice thing about adding these displays to

your device is that you will only need to work with two connections. You just need to work with a ribbon cable that will connect back to the DSI port and power from the GPIO port. The touchscreen is able to support up to 10 finger touch, depending on the type of screen you try to work with.

The Raspberry Pi CanaKit

This is a nice thing to add to your list if you are looking for more accessories to add. This kit is going to come with a variety of components that you can work with. And when you order it, you will find that it comes in a white cardboard box that is plain and filled with equipment. And it is also going to contain a black plastic case to go with your device. Some of the other things that come in this kit, along with a Raspberry Pi 3 device, includes:

- The resistor and GPI color quick reference cards
- Heat sink
- 32GB Micro SD card (a class 10 option)
- HDMI cable
- A USB Wi-Fi adapter
- 2.5A power supply
- CanaKit General Assembly Guide
- CanaKit General Guide for Beginners to Electronic Components
- Five 10K Ohm resistors
- 10 by 220 Ohm Resistors
- 2 push button switches
- 2 blue LEDs
- 2 yellow LEDs
- 2 green LEDs
- 2 red LEDs
- RGB LED
- 10 M/F jumper wires
- 32 M/M jumper wires

- Full-size large breadboard
- GPIO Ribbon cable
- CanaKit GPIO-to-Breadboard interface board

As you can see in this kit, there are even a few of the things and accessories that we have discussed in this chapter already. This is a very popular kit on the market, and it comes with a good warranty on it, as long as you purchase from a good and reputable seller. This can be a good option to work with if you are a beginner to using the Raspberry Pi 3 and you want to make sure that you are using it in the proper manner to get the best benefits.

These are just a few of the different options that you have available when it comes to adding some accessories to your Raspberry Pi 3 device. These are going to be great for ensuring that you can get the most out of this device, and really learn a part of the programming that comes from it. With that said, when you are looking for a good accessory to add to your device, make sure that you are able to pick out options that are compatible with the device that you have, ones that are high quality, and ones that will work for the projects that you are trying to create.

Chapter 14: The LED Project

The next project that we are going to take a look at is the LED project. This is a great one to work with when it comes to creating something with other components coming near it. In order to get started with this project, you will need a few items like:

- A breadboard
- Two male to female jumper wires
- 330-ohm resistor
- An LED

The breadboard is important here because it is going to provide you with a way to connect your electronic components, and you will not have to solder them together and risk some damage to the device. When we use them to test the design of a circuit before we can create a printed circuit board or a PCB—the holes of the breadboard are going to be connected in a certain pattern.

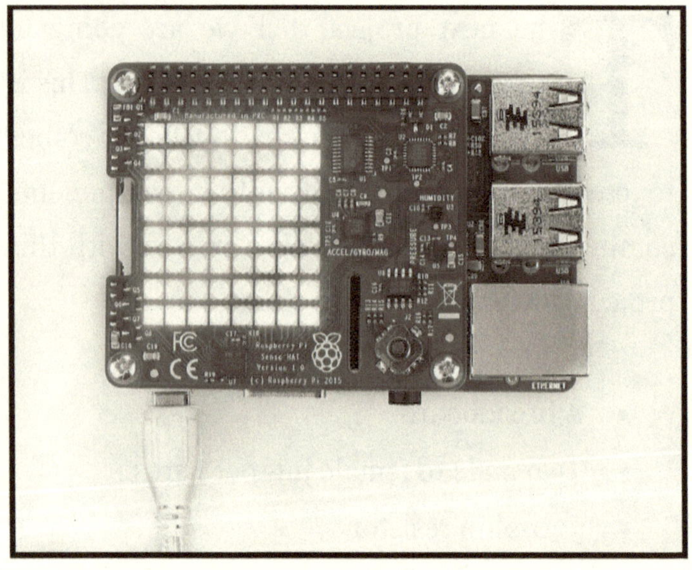

Source: Raspberry Pi with Sense HAT [ONLINE]. Available at: https://commons.wikimedia.org/wiki/File:Raspberry_Pi_with_Sense_HAT.jpg [Accessed 02 April 2019]

The holes that are in the top row will be connected together. The same is going to apply to the holes that we find in the second row, and in the final two rows of the breadboard as well. When we look at the center area, there are going to be two blocks of five lines of holes each. The holes of each of these columns in every line will be connected as well. This may seem a bit strange when you are getting things set up, but this setup is going to be convenient when you want to design a circuit for prototyping.

The LED, or the Light Emitting Diode, will light when you get the electricity to pass through it. After you select the LED that you want to work with, you may notice that there is going to be one leg that is longer than the other one. The longer leg is going to be known as the anode, and it needs to be connected to the positive supply on the circuit. With the shorter leg, known as the cathode, you will need to connect to the negative side.

For this project, the LED is only going to work for you if you supply the power in the right order. If you end up going against the directions at some point and you connect them in the wrong way, the lights are going to fail. However, even though the light does fail and won't show up, it is not going to break them. This is a good way to test whether you are doing it the right way.

The resistors are going to be used when it is time to connect the LEDs to the GPIO pins on the device. Your Raspberry Pi 3 device is only able to supply a bit of current to the lights. It won't be able to supply a ton, usually around 60 mA.

In most situations, the LED is going to need some more power than this, and this means that they could burn up the Pi device. The purpose of working with the resistors in the circuit is to make sure that only a small current passes, and that your device isn't going to get damaged in the process. In this case, we are going to work with resistors that are 300 ohms, ones that are identified by their color codes to help make it easier.

And finally, you will need to work with some jumper wires to finish this project. These are going to be used on the breadboard in order to jump from one connection over to the next. You will be using those with different kinds of connectors at their ends.

Building the Circuit

At this point, we are going to work on building up our circuit. The circuit is going to be made up of the power supply, which will come from your Pi device, the LED, which is going to light up for you to see once the power passes through it, and a resistor for limiting how much power flows through the circuit.

One of the ground pins that you need to have will be used in order to act as the negative ends, or the 0, of the battery. A GPIO pin is going to provide us with the positive end of the battery that we need. In this case, we are going to use pin 18 on the breadboard. What this means is that if it is taken high, the volts are going to be 3.3 and the LED lights are going to show up.

In the next step, you can just turn off the Pi device if you happen to cause a short on something on accident. You should use one of the jumper wires in order to connect the ground pin back to the rail, which is marked with the color blue on the headboard. The corresponding female end is then going to the pin of the Pi device. On the other hand, the male one is going to go to the hole on your breadboard.

At this point, the resistor should then be connected to the same row on the breadboard to a column. You can then take the legs of the LED and have them pushed into the breadboard to a column while ensuring that the right leg ends up on the right. You are then able to complete the circuit by making a connection of pin 18 to the right of your LED's right side leg.

Writing the Program

At this point, it is time to create a bit of code to ensure that you are able to actually send the electricity to the LED light and turn it on. To do this, you can turn on the device, then launch your terminal. You should first start this out by creating a new file named "*LED.py*". Once that is all set up, you can type in the code below to your terminal:

```
nano LED.py
        import RPi.GPIO as GPIO
import time
```

```
GPIO.setmode(GPIO.BCM)
GPIO.setwarnings(False)
GPIO.setup(18,GPIO.OUT)

        Print "LED is on"
GPIO.output(19,GPIO.HIGH)

        Time.sleep(1)

        Print "LED is off"
GPIO.output(18,GPIO.LOW)
```

After the code has been typed and checked, you can save it, and then exit the text editor by pressing on CTRL + x and Y and hit the Enter key. When you are ready to run the code in the file that you just saved, you simply need to type the following command on the terminal "*sudo python LED.py*"

As you do this, you should observe how the LED

behaves. You will see that the light is going to turn on for a second, and then it will blink off. In case you do end up getting an error, know that you have an error that occurs in the code at this point. So what you want to do is go to your nano text editor and then check the code to see if there are any errors that you see.

The statement of "*import RPi.GPIO as GPIO*" is going to help make sure that the GPIO library is imported to the device so that you are able to get the code to execute the way that you want. Then, there needs to be a pause in the script—and you will need to use the statement "*import time*" so that the time library is there to help us achieve it.

There are also a few different names that come with some of the pins that we are using—the "*GPIO.BCM*" statement is going to tell the Python interpreter the kind of numbering system that you want to be able to use. And then we need to use the "*GPIO.setwarnings(False)*" statement to ensure that we are able to turn off the feature that usually happens for printing out any warning messages on the screen.

Since we just want to make sure that we are just looking at the lights, and not looking at the screen really for this project, it is not necessary to have anything, even an error message, show up on the screen. Instead, you will be able to tell there is an error based on if the light shows up or not. If the light doesn't show up, then we know that the project didn't work. If the light does blink, then the code worked.

The statement of "*GPIO.setup*" is used to help us to tell the interpreter that a pin at number 18 has to be used to help us display the information. Then the statement of "*print LED is on*" has to be used here in order to show us a message on the screen.

The statement of "*GPIO.output*" can help us turn on our GPIO pin. This is an indication that our pin has been made to provide the power of 3.3 volts. This voltage is enough to turn the LED light on. The "*time.sleep(1)*" will help us to make sure that the Python program paused for a second. And the next line is going to be simple as it helps print some information on the screen.

The statement of "*GPIO.output*" is going to help out because it will make sure that the GPIO pin is turned off, which means that this pin is not going to supply the power to the LED light any longer. At this point, if you have seen the light go up, you know that you have achieved your target. This is going to help you to turn the LED on and off.

Chapter 15: Creating a Photo Frame

The next project that we are going to take a look at is how to turn the Raspberry Pi 3 into a photo frame. This is a good one to help you to view the photos of your loved ones—or really anything that you would like to display. This chapter is going to take some time to help you create a digital photo frame. The things that you are going to need in this project include:

- USB mouse
- Raspberry Pi case
- USB keyboard
- Screen (a touchscreen is the best option if you can find one)
- Wi-Fi dongle or an Ethernet cable

- A USB drive or external hard drive
- A micro SD card
- Raspberry Pi 3

We are going to use the touch screen for Raspberry Pi, but feel free to make use of any screen you have. You only have to connect the Pi 3 to the screen via the DSI port, HDMI port, or a custom HAT if you would like. But first, we need to go through and set up the software to create our photo frame.

Our first setting is going to involve preventing the screen from going blank. This is going to require us to implement a power setting on the PI 3. The feature that makes the screen go off should be changed in the "*lightdm.conf*" file. You can use the code "*sudo nano /etc/lightdm/lightdm.conf*" in order to open up the file. The file is then going to be opened up with the help of your nano editor. You can identify the line of [SeatsDefaults], then add the statement below to it "*xserver-command=X -s 0 -dpms*". You can then press on CTRL + X and then Y to exit out of the file.

Now, you need to take some time to reboot the device. When you do this, you will see that the screen is not going to turn off, even if you haven't been using it for 10 minutes or more. The device can be rebooted back up when you use the command of "*sudo reboot*".

Now, you may need to take some time to set it up so that you can drag and drop images into the Pi 3 device. In this case, you will need to set up your own network attached storage. When you do this, you will be able to set up your "s" folder that you will then be able to find on the local network. It is also a good idea for you to set up SSH or the Secure Shell so that you are able to access the device, even if the slideshow continues.

One thing to note here is that you don't really have an easy way to exit the slideshow with your Raspberry Pi photo frame, unless you go through and choose to turn the device on and off, and you don't have it start automatically.

When you are ready to set up the slideshow, we are going to use the "*feh*" package to help. This is a good cataloguer and an image viewer that can work well with this device. This image viewer is nice because it is not going to be bogged down, even if you are working with some dependencies in GUI that are huge. We like this one because there aren't any big complications that come with this program, and it is considered pretty lightweight. To help you install this package, you can use the following command "*sudo apt-get install feh*".

At this point, you will need to take some time to check out whether this package is working the way that is expected. You can achieve this by running the command that we have below. Note, remember that the *"/media/NICDD1/test"* should be replaced with the directory where you have stored the image. The command that you can work with is:

DISPLAY=:0.0
XAUTHORITY=/home/pi/.Xauthority/usr/bin/feh-quiet-preload—randomize—full-screen—reload 60 -Y -slideshow-delay 15.0/media/NICDD1/test

We are now able to make the command shorter as well. You will notice at this time that the command line bar is going to be locked because you have typed a long-running command. If you want to work with the background, you can just type the & sign.

We should now go ahead and store it in some

kind of script file. This can be added, or you can change it up later on. The file can be made when you run the command of "*sudo nano/home/pi/picture-frame.sh*". In this case, we went through and named the file "*picture-frame.sh*" and then you want to work with the command of:

#!/bin/bash

DISPLAY=0.0
XAUTHORITY=/home/pi/Xauthortiy/usr/bin/f
eh -q-p -Z -F -R 60 -Y =D
15.0/media/NICCD1/test

At this point, it is time for you to run the script to test whether or not it is working. You can do this by running the following command "*hash/home/pi/picture-frame.sh*" We need to make sure that this script starts to begin during your boot time. This ensures that the slideshow is going to work when you want. Since you have this SSH enabled, it is possible to access the Pi from a locate location, even if you are somewhere that you can't touch the GUI or the screen. You will be able to do this before the boot time. You can run the following command in order to help you run the "*rc.local*" file: "*sudo nano/etc/rc.local*"

From here, you are able to identify the "*exit 0*" command and then use the command of "*sleep 10 bash/home/picture-frame.sh &*".

At this point, you have the slideshow ready-to-go. The slideshow should begin on the Raspberry Pi once you turn it on, and will keep running until you go through and exit it!

Chapter 16: Installing a Magic Mirror on the Raspberry Pi 3

The next project that we are going to look at is installing Magic Mirror on your device. This is going to refer to a webpage that is able to make sure that a web server can show up on the device. The items that you will need to start this project include:

- HDMI cable
- A microSD card that is at least 32 GB
- A microSD card reader
- A power supply for Raspberry Pi that is 2A
- USB mouse

When you are ready to get started with this project, make sure that the Raspbian OS is already on your Pi device. This will ensure that you are able to run the MagicMirror and Jasper on it. Raspbian Jessy is going to be best for what we are doing in this chapter, but other versions can work as well. If you want to work with Raspbian Jessy, you can get the image of it from the archives, and then burn it over your SD card.

Now that you have placed the right operating system on your SD card, you can unplug it from the computer and plug it into the Raspberry Pi. Connect the mouse, the HMI cable, power cable, keyboard, and the Wi-Fi USB adapter to get it all ready. If you are going to use the shell instead of using the command line, you just need to type the command of "*startx*" into the GUI to start.

When you are trying to use MagicMirror, it is going to expect that the Wi-Fi is enabled on the

Pi in order to work. This is important because it will allow the connection to the Internet, and makes it easier for you to access the device remotely if you need. From here, you can click on the network icon that is found on the top right corner of the screen. Choose the Wi-Fi that you want to use, type in the password that goes with the Wi-Fi connection and then click OK.

Once you have this part set up, you are able to work on setting up a remote connection back to the Pi from your computer. You will need to launch the command prompt or the terminal either from your Windows computer or your Mac system and type in the command "*ssh pi@your-pis-ip-address*" if you are asked to enter the password at this point, you need to type in the default password that goes with your Raspberry Pi device.

Now it is time to go through and configure the

Raspbian operating system. It is always a good idea to change the password that is on the Pi device. To do this, you just need to type in the following command before hitting the enter key "*passwd*". The filesystem that is with your Pi should expand so that you are able to fill up all of the space that is available and boot into the GUI as you need.

To make this happen, you will use the following command "*sudo raspi-config*". You can press enter and then choose to expand the FileSystem and then press the enter key again. In the next step, we are going to use the Pi in order to boot ourselves into the Raspbian GUI for the Chromium kiosk mode. To make this happen, we need to click on Enable Boot to Desktop Scratch. Then, we need to select the Desktop Log In. Highlight the choice that you want, and then use the Tab to get to them. Press the Enter Key. Tab your way over to it, hit Enter, and then reboot the device by using the right command.

The next thing that we need to concentrate on is installing chromium. This is going to be a web browser that you can configure and get it to run just like a kiosk. This is a good thing to do is to provide the interface for Magic Mirror. We then need to take some time to download and install the necessary packages. If you are working with the Wheezy version, you need to run with the following command:

sudo apt-get install chromium x11-xserver-utils unclutter

Next, you need to install Apache into here. The dashboard that you are going to work with for Magic Mirror is a web page. This means that you will need to have some kind of web server to host this dashboard. This is going to call for us to install the Apache server and we can do this with the following command "*sudo apt-get install apache2 apache2-doc apache2-utils*".

Then you can do the following command in order to make sure that you have the right support that is needed for PHP "*sudo apt-get install libapache2-mod-php5 php5 php-pear php5 -xcache*". To make sure that this takes effect the way that you want, you need to do the reboot command in order to get the Raspberry Pi set up. After the Pi reboots, you will know that all of the changes you just made are going to be in effect.

Now we need to work with installing the interface in the right way. There are several types of dashboards that you can use when it comes to Magic Mirror. However, you only need to work with one, so now we are going to go ahead and install it. To change to the webroot directory, you will need the code of "*cd /var/www*". If you are working with the Jessie format, you will be able to get the web root at "*/var/www/html*".

We now need to go through and clone the MichMich's MagicMirror Repository. The command that you need in order to achieve this is "*sudo it clone https://github.com/MichMich/MagicMirror.git*". This is going to make sure that we have the right dashboard that we need to use.

You can then continue through a few more commands that come up on the screen, and the MagicMirror is going to be installed on your system!

Chapter 17: Troubleshooting Your Raspberry Pi Device

The last topic that we are going to explore in this guidebook is some of the ways that you can fix the device if it is not working properly for you. When you get this device into your own home, you are likely to notice that there are a lot of cool things that come with it. It is a very strong computer that can perform a lot of cool things—things that you wouldn't expect considering how different and how much smaller it is to a traditional computer.

Here, we are going to take a look at some of the issues that could come up when you are working on your Raspberry Pi. The thing to remember here is that the only thing that is really wrong with the Raspberry Pi, at least 99 percent of the time, is you. Unless you have been really unlucky and received a dud from the company, the issues that you are now dealing with are going to be more than likely due to the power supply to the device, problems that come with the SD card that you are trying to use, or an issue with incorrect cabling.

The good news is that these common issues are ones that you are able to fix pretty easily. You can simply reset the device, replace the parts, or start over. These issues are so simple that most people worry that they are missing out on something when they just focus on these issues, and then they will keep looking for something that is more of a challenge—assuming that those have to be the reason for the failure.

However, for the most part, when the Raspberry Pi device is not working the way that it should, it really is because of an issue that is small. We are going to take a look at some of these common issues and how you can try to avoid them—thus ensuring in the process that you are able to get the most out of your Raspberry Pi device.

Ways to Avoid an SD Card That Is Corrupted

One of the most common problems that you are going to run into when working with the Raspberry Pi device is that the SD card you choose to work with is corrupted. Now, this usually isn't going to be something that you have to deal with that much if you plan to work with an SD card that has been designed to be written on regularly. But sometimes the older SD cards are going to get corrupted fast, which manes that your operating system for the Pi device is not going to be able to boot properly.

When you are picking out an SD card for this device, make sure that you go with one that is brand new, rather than pulling one out of the closet and hoping that it will work. You want to go with one that is rated high, one that is SDHC and holds onto at least 2GB or more. The Pi device is going to use storage similar to what you see with an Ultrabook or a high-end tablet. This means that you want to make sure that it is strong enough, sturdy enough, and has enough storage for the memory on it.

However, no matter which of the SD cards you choose to use, there are also other methods that can corrupt the data here. The first one is when you try to remove the SD card while your device is up and running. Just like with a USB storage device when you use it on a Windows PC, you should only remove the storage device when it is safe to do so. And for the Raspberry Pi device, it is only safe to remove the card when the device has had time to shut down completely.

Another issue comes up when you are trying to switch the device off in an incorrect manner. To make sure that you are shutting down the Pi device in the safe and effective manner, and to avoid any issues with corrupting the card, or any of the other issues that may come up, you will need to open up the command line and type in the command "*sudo shutdown -h now*".

How to Avoid Relying on Only the Main Power

The fact that the Raspberry Pi device is going to use a USB mains adaptor for power can lead you into almost a false sense of security when you are using it, especially when it comes to sending power over to the device. After all, the USB ports are things that you are able to find on regular Pcs, and on some desktop monitors, so why not use one of these connectors in order to help you to provide power to this small computer.

However, it is important to realize that the whole power thing is not going to be as simple as this. While it is possible that your device is going to be able to receive enough power when you use a USB 2.0 port to boot up and to run, running the processor intensive tasks, or powering a USB network connection, USB storage, a mouse, and a keyboard will probably prove too much for this kind of power source. If the Pi shuts down right after booting, then it is likely that the small computer is not receiving the amount of power that it needs to run successfully.

The best way to work with this issue is to only power the device when you have the right kind of power adaptor to help. There are several options available for you to use here, and you just need to pick out the one that works with your preference.

Checking out the Cables That You Are Using

Another important thing that you can work with on the Raspberry Pi is to keep your eye on the cabling. This is especially important if you plan to use one of the cases that are custom and are available. There are times when manufacturing problems are going to come up with the cables and the cases, and when these do happen, they are going to lead us to deal with incorrect seating of power. You may also find that the HDMI cables and the Ethernet cables that you choose can lead to these problems as well.

In a similar manner, you also need to be aware that sometimes the adaptors that you will want to go with are going to be cheaply made, and they may not work the way that you want to provide power or to work with the other parts of the device. You should be careful when purchasing parts on eBay and Amazon because you may not be getting the amount of power and more that you are looking for. And when you get an adaptor or a wire cable that is cheaply made and isn't really compatible with the Raspberry Pi that you are using, this is going to lead to a lot of issues.

For example, the VGA and HDMI cables and adaptors might claim to be usable, and the seller may have made some big promises to the same tune, but faults can easily arise. And when these faults do happen, it is going to put both the Raspberry Pi device and your HDTV or monitor at a great deal of risk. This is why you need always to be careful about the extra adaptors and such that you choose to purchase. You want to make sure that you pick ones that are going to work, ones that will provide you with the amount of power that you need, but won't risk the Raspberry Pi device or any of the other components that you are using with it.

Another thing to be aware of here is the USB cables. The USB cables that are designed to work with charging your smartphone may not be suitable for powering your Raspberry Pi device. This is true whether or not the main adaptor has been connected in the right place.

Basically, there is a lot of damage and issues that can come up when you use the wrong adaptors and cables with your Raspberry Pi device. This may seem easy enough to understand, but make sure that you are going with products that work well, products that match up to the device, and ones that aren't too cheaply made.

If you are working with a Raspberry Pi device, you should be certain that as with most of the desktop computers that you choose to work with, everything needs to be connected in the right manner. Before you even boot up the device for the first tie, make sure that you go through and double-check and confirm that you have all of the necessary storage media, peripherals, and cables in place and then you can start.

For the most part, the steps that we just talked about are going to be enough to ensure that any time your Raspberry Pi device stops working how it should, you will be able to get it fixed and up and running in no time—and when you follow these steps and are careful about the way that you treat your device, you can save a lot of time and money when it comes to dealing with data corruption or re-imaging your SD card.

Conclusion

There are a lot of changes that come with working in the field of technology, and there are a lot of cool projects that you can work within this field to make one of your own items and projects. However, to get started, you have to know the basics of programming and coding. Many beginners are going to take a look at most options for programming and feel like the whole thing is overwhelming and too hard to work with. They may feel hopeless and like they will never be able to learn how to do the work at all.

The good news is that Raspberry Pi 3, as well as the other products in the Raspberry Pi, will help even a beginner to learn how to code and program. There are a lot of different operating systems and coding languages that you are able to choose from when working on this device, and you are going to be able to see the results in no time.

This guidebook took some time to explore more about Raspberry Pi 3 and what you are able to do with it. We will look at what this device is all about, how to turn it on and get the operating system set up on it, and even some of the projects that you are able to create with the help of the Raspbian operating system and the Python coding language. You will quickly see that the Raspberry Pi device is such a good one to work with—and in no time, you will be creating your own media center, your own phone, and even your own arcade. And all it takes is the Raspberry Pi device, a few accessories, and a few simple codes to make it happen.

There is so much that comes with the idea of the

Raspberry Pi device. But before we can start to create some of the great codes and programs that you read about in this book, we needed to spend some time exploring this device, and all that it can do. Many beginners may see this small computer device and feel worried that it will be too complicated for them. But because it works on so many different systems, accepts a wide variety of coding languages, and can do so many things, you will find that it is easier to learn at your own speed, and in your own way, compared to some of the other methods.

Whether you want to explore your current knowledge about technology to include the Raspberry Pi family, or you are a beginner who wants to start from scratch, these devices are the perfect place for you to start.

There are a lot of neat things that you can do when it comes to using any of the Raspberry Pi versions, but the Raspberry Pi 3 is one of the best. Make sure to read through this guidebook to help you learn more about this device and all of the cool things that you are able to do with the Raspberry Pi 3.

www.ingramcontent.com/pod-product-compliance
Lightning Source LLC
La Vergne TN
LVHW091410190726
843491LV00006B/1359

* 9 7 8 3 9 0 3 3 3 1 3 2 7 *